Night work

Night work

Its effects on the health and welfare of the worker

J. Carpentier
P. Cazamian

International Labour Office   Geneva

ISBN 92-2-101676-5 (limp cover)
ISBN 92-2-101729-X (hard cover)

First published 1977

Printed by Presses Centrales Lausanne, Switzerland

PREFACE

At its 191st Session in November 1973 the Governing Body of the International Labour Office considered the replies of governments concerning a draft report on the application of the Night Work (Women) Convention (Revised), 1948 (No. 89), and of the corresponding Conventions of 1934 and 1919 (Nos. 41 and 4). The sense of the many opinions expressed both in the replies received from governments and in the course of the Governing Body's discussion was that the problems which were the subject of those Conventions should continue to be studied so that, on the basis of fuller information on the various aspects of those problems, the Governing Body might decide whether the revision of the standards laid down in the Conventions was desirable. The Governing Body accordingly decided to request the Director-General to initiate a thorough examination of the various questions raised and to submit the matter again to the Governing Body as soon as possible. The present study, which is concerned with the effects of night work on individuals, especially from the physiological and psychological points of view, as well as with the community, family and social aspects of night work, gives effect to that decision. It has been prepared by two leading authorities in this field: James Carpentier,[1] who is responsible for the general introduction, and Dr. Pierre Cazamian,[2] who, with the collaboration of Catherine Delgrange, François Hubault and Jacques Guérin, is responsible for the remainder of the study.

The temporal organisation of occupational activities raises problems relating, in particular, to the duration of work, the rhythm or intensity of the activities, the development of working capacities and of employment and working life, the duration of periods of rest and of holidays and the choice of work schedules. The last-mentioned question has itself several facets, among

---

[1] Adviser on ergonomics to the European Centre of Human Ecology, University of Geneva.

[2] Associate Professor at the University of Paris I.

them work in successive shifts, either regular or rotating, and night work. It is the latter form of work that is the subject of the present study.

Broadly speaking, night work is practised in one or other of two ways, depending on the nature of the work: either regularly and excluding all other work schedules, as in the case of night watchmen, or within a system of successive shifts, which may be rotating or regular, as in the case of continuous process industries. Studies of night work are consequently often confused with studies of team work. In that event it becomes difficult to isolate the effects that are specific to, respectively, rotating shifts, the particular shift and regular night shifts. The present study will report, therefore, the findings both of studies of shift work in so far as they are concerned also with night work and of studies relating directly or exclusively to night work alone.

Shift work has already been the subject of a study prepared for the International Labour Office by Marc Maurice,[1] which reviewed all the technical, economic, physiological, psychological and social problems, as well as the problems of regulations and of practice, which shift work raises.

Whereas the number of workers employed under the various systems of shift work continues to expand, reaching in 1974 between 15 and 25 per cent of the economically active population in the industrialised countries, the practice of the continuous work system (that is, including a night shift) is developing even more rapidly. It is estimated that nearly one-half of the workers now employed on shift work have to work at night, while the practice of regular night work, in respect of which published statistics are not available, is probably also spreading. Thus in the industrialised countries the practice of night work is being extended continuously and at a pace which has been accelerating in the course of the past decade.

Furthermore, industrialisation, followed by automation, which had been confined for many years to certain regions, is now being extended to many other parts of the world. This development—which, it can be foreseen, will gather speed—is bringing to these other regions a sudden and widespread practice of night work.

The Governing Body of the International Labour Office is well aware of the implications of this increasing recourse to night work, which raises a series of questions, including the following:

— Is night work medically harmful, whether to women workers only or to all workers ?

— Is it acceptable from the social point of view ?

— Is it economically necessary and warranted ?

— Should it be made the subject of special regulations ?

---

[1] Maurice (1975). The authors have endeavoured to provide references to the works and articles which they have consulted. A bibliography arranged alphabetically by authors' names is given at the end of the book. In the body of the study, the references are given in footnotes in the usual abridged form (author's name and year of publication).

The effects of night work on the health of workers and on family and social life now seem to be sufficiently well established, thanks to advances in general knowledge of biological rhythms and sleep and in more specialised knowledge of the practice and pathology of shift work at night. It is consequently possible to assess those effects, to explain certain attitudes and to point to possible measures and regulations. The new knowledge also makes it possible to isolate the medical aspects of the question and thus to discern the role played by the economic, sociological and policy factors in the decisions taken.

In the economic field, the data obtained from investigations and the established facts are still fragmentary and not easy to present systematically, while such conclusions as can be reached depend on the particular and varying situation of individual undertakings and countries. Moreover, the study on shift work referred to above, which the International Labour Office published in 1975, dealt in large measure with its economic aspects, which are substantially comparable or even identical to the economic aspects of night work.

It has therefore seemed preferable for the time being to confine the scope of the main part of this study to the first two questions: the physiological, psychological and medico-pathological aspects of night work, and the family and social aspects. However, this limitation will not preclude consideration also of the last question, that of the possible need for regulations. There will be some reference to that question in the introduction and in the conclusions.

The introduction is designed to draw attention to some of the main problems of night work. It refers to the technical, economic and social factors which determine recourse to night work and the human and social implications of that work.

The first two chapters, which constitute the core of the study, describe the knowledge that has been acquired concerning night work and its effects on the worker, his family and the community, and examine the psychological, physiological and medico-pathological aspects of those effects and the family and social aspects. The third chapter presents some comments and recommendations of an ergonomic character concerning the organisation of shift work, the recommendations being based on the considerations set out in the two preceding chapters. A brief general conclusion sets out the main findings and their implications concerning the necessary protection of the worker.

An extensive summary of this study was submitted to the Governing Body at its 198th Session in November 1975. On the basis of that summary and of other documents submitted to it, the Governing Body requested the Director-General to arrange for the available documentary material to be completed in the light of recent studies and developments in member States. A tripartite meeting of experts may be convened in the near future to consider the desirability and form of a new international standard relating to the night work of men and of women.

CONTENTS

INTRODUCTION

In this introduction a number of questions relating to night work will be examined, in the following order: present situation; factors determining recourse to night work; effects of night work on health; effects on employment; economic and social costs and benefits of night work; regulation of night work.

CURRENT ASPECTS OF THE PROBLEM OF NIGHT WORK

In the industrialised countries there have been large increases in the numbers of night workers. The rate of increase has accelerated during the past ten years and the total number of these workers has doubled in 20 years. Depending on the country, night workers account for 8 to 15 per cent of the economically active population. As a result of that growth there have been substantial increases in the number of workers who have become unfit for night work. In many cases the number of these workers is so large that it is not possible to transfer them to other work in undertakings practising night work owing to a lack of normal daytime jobs that would ensure for them the same level of earnings.

At the same time, attitudes have changed, especially with the arrival of young workers on the employment market and with the extension of night work to tertiary sectors requiring employees of a higher social and occupational level.

While the health problem continues to cause concern, there is a growing awareness of the occupational, personal and social difficulties caused by night work. It is noted, too, that the award of financial advantages to compensate for the harm done to health and for the inconveniences in family and social life is inadequate: it does not alleviate the workload of night workers; it distorts attitudes and decisions; and it creates situations that impede the adoption of solutions. Workers and their families show some reluctance to accept the strains of night work. The problems faced by the worker and the undertaking thus become problems for the whole community. In view of the number of workers and families concerned, it is recognised that it is becoming necessary to find social and institutional remedies. Moreover, the growth in the number of women workers in industry raises problems of equality and non-discrimination in the choice of jobs and the development of careers of work—problems which lead to a re-examination of the difference of situation between men and women under night work regulations.

In many countries now undergoing industrialisation an acceleration of development can be expected; in some cases this is even occurring already. These countries are being increasingly faced with the same problems as industrialised countries, but with two aggravating factors: first, a considerable shortening of the process of social transformation, which will add to the difficulties of planning and adaptation and will magnify the consequences; and second, the large size of both the male population and—especially—the female population who will be involved in a development which, by appreciably modifying the traditional standards of life and culture, will have particularly significant family and social consequences. Furthermore, while the severity of the problems and awareness of them have grown,[1] the theoretical and practical knowledge required for their solution has advanced, whether in the case of general knowledge of the physiology of human biological rhythms and of sleep or in the case of observations of the practical consequences of night work, its pathology and its family and social consequences. It has thus become possible to adopt definite attitudes towards the practical measures or regulations demanded by the various parties affected. The problem is no longer confined solely to the relations between employer and worker, who are no longer in full control of solutions: the problem is now one for society as a whole. As such, it must be tackled in relation to its effects on the community and to the standards or aims of society; its solution by methods adapted to national conditions and usages depends on a national and international consensus.[2] These requirements are reflected in the variety of national and international action: symposia of scientific associations concerned with ergonomics and occupational health; studies by occupational organisations; scientific, governmental and international publications; social movements and collective bargaining.

FACTORS DETERMINING RECOURSE TO NIGHT WORK

Any analysis of the technical, economic, organisational and social factors which exercise an influence on the practice of night work is unavoidably artificial because these factors are interdependent, vary with the passage of time and relate to differing situations. For example, the automation of a process can at one point reduce the need for night staff but at the same time increase the technical need to keep sectors situated above or below that point

---

[1] Landier and Vieux (1976); Carpentier and Wisner (1976).

[2] Carpentier and Wisner (1976).

in continuous operation, thereby requiring the recruitment of more workers for night work.

These factors may refer not only to purely economic purposes of profitability or profit but also to social aims such as the need to provide as many jobs as possible with the equipment available, to increase the productivity of investments designed to raise a country's economic level and to furnish the production required for the welfare and protection of the population. Moreover, the national interest or national defence may be, in certain circumstances, at stake.

Social factors

Individual or social demand for continuous provision of certain services (including, in particular, those of the police, security services and hospitals) is also a strongly compelling factor. The protection of the community is no doubt a sign of progress but the growth of the services' needs may be open to question. Certain kinds of regional development and town planning seem to increase the need for supervision and action. The demand of the community for information, transport, food and leisure may not always justify the subjection of workers to abnormal working conditions in order to satisfy the consumers.

One of the socio-economic factors is the interest that the community, public opinion and influential groups may come to show in an intensification of certain outputs or in the continuous provision of certain services. Yet from an over-all point of view (as, for example, that of world food, health and educational needs) there might be a very different set of priorities under which the need for the uninterrupted provision of certain goods and services could become questionable.

Social and economic factors appear to play an increasingly decisive role in the adoption of night work. Indeed, an OECD group of experts reached the conclusion in 1974 that the methods of competition practised at the world level caused society to accept and promote shift work, regarding it as a necessity yet without necessarily seeing in it any advantages either for particular undertakings or for the community. The world-wide nature of that competition and its generally recognised baneful social consequences led that group to advocate the suppression of night work by means of a voluntary international agreement.

Some writers consider also that the socio-economic aspects of night work is becoming crucial. They point out that, while some external benefits, such as a reduction of certain peak costs (demand for electricity, use of transport) can be of importance to the community, "external costs are more difficult to define. The most important may be the loss to the community because the shift worker, as compared to the day worker, cannot make a full contribution to the community outside his workplace, but should shift working become more widespread the external costs may become increasingly significant." [1]

---

[1] National Board for Prices and Incomes (United Kingdom) (1970), para. 201.

While there are some social factors which may conduce to the practice of night work, there are also some that operate against it.[1] An increasingly reserved attitude towards night work is in fact being adopted in some labour quarters. This reserve can be noted first of all on the part of trade union organisations which take the view that "health is not for sale" and that family and social life must be preserved; but it is also an attitude that is being increasingly adopted by young workers belonging to the higher social and occupational levels, who view with concern the rapid extension of night work to tertiary sectors calling for advanced skills and mental work. It can be noted also in some managements of rapidly expanding undertakings which, having recruited large numbers of workers for night shifts during the past 20 years, are faced with difficulties in transferring to other work a growing number of workers who have become unfit for night work at an age that becomes all the earlier as the physical and mental workload of the night shifts tends to become heavier.

There has also been a change in attitude towards the financial advantages attached to the practice of night work. These advantages, which have largely accounted for the extension of night work, are still of decisive importance in the recruitment of the labour force needed for the less attractive jobs. They are advantages that appeal to many workers. Nevertheless, they have a distorting effect on situations and attitudes and, in many cases, stand in the way of the application of technical and medical measures relating to selection, supervision and transfer to other jobs. The present tendency is to regard them as inappropriate and, to some extent, unacceptable in principle, on the ground that only some compensation of a physiological nature can remedy the physiological drawbacks of night work.

Furthermore, the crowding of the environment and the limitation of the available resources are causing time to be viewed as the last "dimension" that remains available. The abundance of consumer goods that rapidly become obsolete means that time has become a scarce commodity relative to material goods. As a result, time and the possibility of using it are becoming criteria of the quality of life and subjects of social demands at the same time as they are becoming a factor of increase in the profitability of investments and hence targets of new pressures. The organisation of time spent at work now plays a role in the life of the community both as a standard for appraising it and as a problem to be solved.

Technical factors

The technical factors spring from the continuous nature of the physical, chemical and operational processes needed if the quality of goods and services is to be guaranteed.

These factors are no doubt particularly compelling; but it is noticeable that, in many cases, the need for the continuous operation of a process reflects

---

[1] See ILO (1975 a); see also Carpentier (1969).

a more or less transitory inadequacy of technology. The greater the progress of science and techniques, the more diverse do the possible solutions of a problem become. Technical and organisational research can then be channelled in two directions: either towards the automation of critical processes so as to eliminate the need for workers; or, on the other hand, towards discontinuity by accelerating, slowing down, stopping and starting up again certain processes or machines so as to limit appreciably the number of workers required during the night. In this connection a clear distinction must be drawn between the continuous operation of production equipment, the organisation of work schedules so as to ensure continuity of that operation, and the subjection of the individual worker to a system of rotating shifts. These three aspects are not necessarily interlinked; and although employers' organisations may insist that it is necessary to keep certain installations in continuous operation, they also recognise that arrangements can be made to limit the pressures and ensure the safety of night work.

Economic factors

In the course of the second period of industrialisation and especially with the introduction of mechanisation and automation, economic factors had a positive influence on decisions to have recourse to night work and on the regulations allowing night work. The influence thus exercised by economic factors was due to the growth of investments in capital equipment and in human and intellectual resources, and to the constantly diminishing periods of utilisation of these means of production and of the depreciation of the equipment. The shortening of these periods is in turn due to an acceleration of technological innovation, which is altering the conditions of competition, and to changes in production brought about by changes in demand under the influence of marketing techniques.

These coercive factors obviously play a role of prime importance to the survival of an undertaking and of the workers depending on it. It might be thought that the decision whether or not to have recourse to shift work and the choice of the system to be adopted should flow from a weighing up of economic and practical calculations. Yet it was found in an investigation that, in the majority of cases examined, "such calculations had not been made" and that "decisions were largely based on managements' intuitions". "This is not to say", add the authors of the investigation, "that the majority of decisions taken are wrong, but equally because of lack of information, it was not possible to prove that they were correct." [1]

Organisational factors

Having at first authorised night work on technical and social grounds and then on economic grounds, the regulations have been further liberalised by taking into account the organisational facilities obtainable from the continuous

---

[1] National Board for Prices and Incomes (United Kingdom) (1970), para. 274.

operation of equipment situated both above and below the point at which continuous work is technically warranted. These organisational factors are very closely linked to the technical and economic factors. Investigations and statistical data show that there is a correlation between continuous work in shifts, including a night shift, and the concentration and automation of production machines, which are themselves related to the growth in the size of undertakings and to the integration of production and management. These are characteristic features of industrial societies and of the rules to which such societies are subject. They reflect economic pressures and competition and are subject to the effects of transfers of technology. A trend towards an increase in shift work and night work is therefore to be expected.

Yet while the technical pressure for continuous operation is tending to strengthen, it is to be noted that continuity does not imply that activities must be evenly distributed among the various work schedules. It will be possible in many cases, without affecting the continuity of operations, to transfer systematically to daytime shifts operations at present entrusted to the night shift, thereby appreciably reducing the numbers of workers required at night.

NIGHT WORK AND HEALTH

The effects of night work on health, which will be examined in the chapters that follow, are to be seen in the biological rhythms of the body, in essential functions such as sleep and nourishment and in occupational, family and social activities. Questions of biological and psychological rhythms and of work schedules arise when the relations between a worker's rhythm of activity, his various individual rhythms and the rhythms of his family, social and general environment are examined.

Workers are becoming increasingly sensitive to the disruptions to which differences between their work schedules and the timetables of their physical and social environment expose them. These disruptions, which are strongly felt at the psychological and sociological levels, also have physiological aspects. It is not immaterial whether one sleeps at night or by day, and the body will resist the changes in its biological rhythms (which are stable and inseparable from the regular rhythms of the psychological and social environment) that will adapt it to irregular hours or to an artificial programming of more and more of the worker's time. Moreover, the biological adjustment, limited though it is, represents only a part, which is not always the main part, of the adjustment required of the worker and of his family and social environment.

In the pathology of night workers, there are some distinguishing characteristics: a delay in the appearance of effects, some of which are permanent (hence the need, in studies of the subject, to take all the necessary methodological precautions); the presence of indirect effects, including, for example, the indirect effect on nervous and digestive disorders of the direct effect of insufficient and disturbed sleep; a wide variety of individual reactions depending on family, material and social situations, from which a "typology of the shift-worker" [1] and a "typology of shift work" [2] can be derived.

While there is a wide variety of reactions and of situations and while it may be difficult to determine whether the cause of observed disorders is night work or the rotation of work shifts or the workload or living conditions, it appears nevertheless to be well established that, from both the physiological point of view and the family and social point of view, night work is harmful to a large majority of workers and is, therefore, to be deprecated.

While some studies have been made of situations prevailing in conditions of environmental isolation (under the sea or in polar regions) and consequently not subject to the alternation of day and night, most of them have been carried out in industrialised countries situated mainly in temperate zones. It would be of interest to study less conventional working conditions and to inquire, for example, whether the effects of night work in tropical countries, allowing for climatic factors, are the same as in temperate regions; whether, in Arctic and Antarctic regions, the rhythms and the quality of sleep vary in accordance with the wide seasonal differences in duration between day and night; and whether the work schedules have the same effects in all seasons.

NIGHT WORK AND EMPLOYMENT

The general data on employment that are at present available [3] show that the rate of increase, both absolute and relative, in the number of female workers employed in the production of goods and services, which is already substantial in the industrialised countries, is likely to accelerate rapidly. The tendency to have recourse to night work and to shift work is liable, therefore, to come under a twofold pressure.

— On the one hand, there is the pressure of the general increase of population. This growth will affect directly the number of persons, both male and female, seeking employment, so that governments and undertakings might be tempted to have recourse to night work in order to increase employment opportunities with the available equipment, while those seeking work might be induced to accept more readily night work or shift work.

— On the other hand, and especially, there is the pressure of industrialisation. In the countries that are already industrialised the ever increasing amount of investment and the growing complexity of techniques seem likely to induce a desire to resort more and more to night work and shift work; the lightening of physical work, the advance in the vocational training of women and their claim to equal rights to employment might then prompt further recourse to women for night work and shift work. In the countries

---

[1] Chazalette (1973).

[2] Wisner, in Carpentier and Wisner (1976).

[3] ILO (1974) and (1975 b).

in process of industrialisation, which are the most important countries in this connection, the requirements of national development and a desire to ensure the best possible rate of employment will probably bring to the employment market large numbers of female workers at present engaged in domestic tasks or on agricultural work and promote recourse to continuous operations and to night work. Hence the importance of the conclusions adopted in June 1976 by the ILO's World Employment Conference, which stressed the need to reach a proper balance between labour-intensive and capital-intensive techniques so as to promote both growth and employment, as well as the satisfaction of basic needs.

It may thus be expected that the problems of female employment and of its competition with male employment will become more acute. That competition will be all the stronger as night work becomes wanted or offered in sectors of skilled work at a high level of wages or income. It therefore seems necessary both to eliminate all discriminatory access to employment liable to create *de facto* inequalities of remuneration and employment and to protect all workers, both men and women, from the consequences of a possible extension of night work and of work in shifts.

ASSESSMENT OF THE ECONOMIC AND SOCIAL COSTS AND BENEFITS OF NIGHT WORK

As will appear below, it is not easy to assess these costs and benefits. There are analytical difficulties, widely varying situations and solutions and differences of opinion on the appropriate criteria of appraisal.

Analytical difficulties

The many parties concerned include: the individual workers and their families, the undertakings which provide the capital and the management of the production equipment and of the distribution of the goods and services, and the social groups of users, consumers, taxpayers and citizens who receive certain benefits but also have to bear their social costs. The interests and aims of these parties are not necessarily uniform, constant and in harmony.

The factors to be analysed are both numerous and interdependent [1] and they vary in significance with place and time. For example, the improvement of employment and production resulting from night work and its concomitant financial advantages may well lead to a rise in the economic level of the individual and of the community. At the same time, it may make it necessary to increase the production of goods and services, thereby causing some dissatisfaction with, on the one hand, work schedules that do not make it possible to take full advantage of the new scope for consumption and, on the other, the baneful resulting effects on health and family life. Furthermore, the assess-

---

[1] Marris (1966); Lidén and Wallander (1959); Wohlin (1970).

ment of the costs and benefits is subject to changes in the costs of the products—costs which generally tend to decrease rapidly as soon as a technique or a product becomes commonplace. A case in point [1] is that of the technology of computers in Sweden. At first computers were so costly that it was economically justified to use them continuously. There is no likelihood today of finding in Sweden many computers that are used continuously.

Moreover, neither the undertaking nor the community is usually able to isolate and identify the facts relating to the various consequences and implications of night work.

Assessment of situations and of solutions

In the field of conditions of work, the theory of social and technical systems requires that the human costs of work organisation and in particular of night work shall be defined and appraised at two successive levels: first, at the level of the intrinsic significance, or absolute value, of the human and social costs; second, at the level of the magnitude of those costs relative to the aims of the various parties concerned. These appraisals will make it possible to choose, among the various technologies available, those whose characteristics will seem to be most conducive to the attainment of the desired objectives.[2] These objectives will vary, of course, with the particular demographic, economic and technological situation, which, in turn, will vary with the country or region considered and will be subject, moreover, to more or less rapid changes.[3]

It follows that a purely economic or technical assessment can refer only to a particular case. Nevertheless, whatever the aims and objects may be, there should be an assessment of the economic significance of night work and, in a more general way, of continuous operations, which necessarily call for night work. That assessment should take account of the human and social costs, that is, of all the adjustments which night work involves for the worker, his family, the undertaking and the community.[4]

Instead of trying to reach final judgements, one should attempt to draw up detailed balance sheets. What are the individual, occupational, family and social consequences of a particular system of work? What significance is to be attached at a particular time and in a particular situation to those consequences, taking into account the social and economic objectives of the individuals and groups concerned? Consideration must be given also to the implications of different time scales: the calculation of the costs pertains to the short term of, for example, annual budgets, while the assessment of the consequences expected or noted pertains to the long term of, for example, the average duration of life in an occupational group.

---

[1] Lindörn (1974).

[2] Hetman (1974); Carpentier (1974).

[3] Kabaj (1968).

[4] Bartoli (1957).

Social and economic standards of assessment

The economic, technological and employment factors to be assessed refer to situations that may undergo rapid changes and to demands for particular goods and services that may arise, so that varying solutions may be required. None the less, the need to protect the physical and mental health of the worker and his family is permanent and must never be underrated.

Attitudes and opinions and, consequently, standards of appraisal may change, however, under the influence of other factors.

These factors include, first of all, the level of industrialisation, the demographic situation, employment requirements, levels of occupational skill and a policy of reduction of inequalities and discriminations. The role played by these factors explains why judgements of night work and resulting attitudes may differ. Yet at the same time economic interdependence and a concern for equalisation of the conditions of competition can promote the adoption of a common stand at the international level, with the implication that particular interests and differences must be integrated into wider general objectives, such as an international distribution of resources and of work and applications of technologies that will be compatible with respect for the cultural and social values specific to each region.[1]

Another factor is the new way of approaching the economic problems. It consists in an ever more pronounced socialisation of work and of financing which is causing public budgets to bear a growing share of the investments and costs of production; hence the need to assess profitability and productivity at the level, not of the undertaking producing the goods and services, but of the community, taking into account the over-all costs and the direct and indirect consequences, especially the social consequences.

Furthermore, "from a social point of view that takes into account living conditions and individual and social aspirations and whatever may be the findings of economic studies, what still has to be considered is whether technical and economic objectives warrant recourse to abnormal conditions of work and living and whether those objectives might not be secured by means of other solutions".[2]

REGULATIONS AND NEGOTIATIONS

In view of the large number of workers at present affected, the regulation of night work can no longer be confined to negative prescriptions applicable to situations regarded as exceptional. There is a desire in some countries for general regulations governing both regular night work and night shifts.

In the field of negotiations and regulations, a twofold movement is at work. It aims at action at a national or even international level, on the one hand, and at negotiations with the undertaking, on the other.

---

[1] Herman (1975); Richta (1969); Club of Rome, Executive Committee (1974).
[2] INRS (1975).

Regulations at the national and international level seem indispensable for the purpose of laying down certain principles and provisions that are of crucial importance in matters such as the respect for night sleep between the hours of 10 p.m. and 5 a.m. Only uniform regulations in such matters can ensure the protection of the workers' health and the equality of conditions of competition. Nevertheless, in view of the diversity of objectives and situations, there must be full freedom of choice. This aim can be fostered through locally negotiated adjustments of the regulations to particular requirements.

PHYSIOLOGICAL, PSYCHOLOGICAL AND MEDICAL EFFECTS OF NIGHT WORK

1

In order to understand fully the problems arising out of working at night, it is necessary first of all to turn to the existing body of general knowledge of physiological activity, of the activity which work entails and of fatigue, with special reference to recently acquired knowledge of biological rhythms. This chapter will open, therefore, with a recapitulation of general information on biological rhythms, on wakefulness and sleep and on work and fatigue.

That review can then be followed by a general survey of the effects of night work on various physiological and psychological indicators or functions, on various indicators of occupational activity and on the pathology of workers.

Lastly, an attempt will be made to determine how reactions to night work are influenced by the nature of the occupation and by certain individual characteristics.

GENERAL REMARKS ON BIOLOGICAL RHYTHMS, WAKEFULNESS AND SLEEP, WORK AND FATIGUE

Biological rhythms

Rhythmic activity is one of the basic properties of living matter. In plant and in animal life there is a cyclical alternation of periods of hyperactivity and of reduced activity. There is thus a complementary dimension of time—a "temporal anatomy", to use Reinberg's expression—to be added to the classic spatial dimension of anatomy. Yet chronobiology, as an autonomous scientific discipline, is of recent origin.[1]

Biological rhythms vary in frequency: one second for the high-frequency periodicity of systems, such as the nervous system, that can be excited; 24 hours for a medium-frequency periodicity; one month (women's ovarian cycle) or one year for low-frequency periodicities. Moreover, rhythms affect all parts

---

[1] For a detailed bibliography of the question, see Reinberg (1974), p. 43. See also Halberg and Howard (1958); Aschoff (1963); Reinberg and Ghata (1964).

of the body: cell, tissue, organs, system of organs and the individual as a whole. Each rhythm having its own autonomic cycle, the rhythm of the body as a whole, though apparently uniform, conceals multiple concurrencies and discordances in the periods of subordinate rhythms. Furthermore, every rhythm, since it can be likened to a sinusoidal function or to the conjugation of several sinusoids, is measurable in terms of several parameters: its duration, its amplitude and its maximum and minimum, from which two terms (which are, moreover, defined by their angle in phase) an adjusted mean level can be derived.

The only rhythms relevant to the subject of this study are those medium-frequency rhythms of the human body to which the descriptors "circadian" (L. *circa* about, *dies* day; about 24 hours) and "nyctohemeral" (that is, with alternating day (Gr. *hemera*) and night (Gr. *nyx*)), are applied.

The circadian rhythms govern many biological variables in the human body as a whole (temperature, pulse, blood pressure), in the brain (electroencephalographic rhythms), in the cardio-respiratory system (breathing rhythm, vital capacity, intake of oxygen), in the blood (cells and chemical composition), in the metabolisms and in the endocrine secretions (hormones dissolved in the plasma and in the urine).

In the usual case of activity by day and rest at night, most of these variables are in maximum activation by day (though with peaks at different hours) and in minimum activation by night. It is as if the body were in a state of activation during daytime and a state of de-activation during the night.

Origin of biological rhythms; their possible entrainment

The origin of circadian rhythms was for a long time a subject of debate. As they coincided with the alternation of day and night and varied with that alternation (as in the case of, for example, transmeridian flights) and as they were not present in the new-born child (who wakens, suckles and sleeps six times in the 24 hours), it was thought at first that they corresponded to reflexes conditioned by the succession of light and darkness, the conditioning being acquired during the first years of life. Today the prevailing opinion is, on the contrary, that these rhythms are hereditary and form part of the genetic heritage of the species, as in the case of most of the other biological rhythms.[1] This opinion has led to the view that "the delay in the appearance of the circadian rhythm in children depends on the maturing of their central nervous systems, not on acquisition or on apprenticeship".[2] It would appear, therefore, that nyctohemeral rhythms—or, more exactly, the social habits of daytime activity and of sleep at night—act only as factors of synchronisation.

At all events, these factors are found to be sufficiently effective for a change in them to bring about a correlative change in the circadian rhythms, though

---

[1] Pittendrigh (1960).
[2] Reinberg and Ghata (1964), p. 104.

only after lapses of time and in degrees varying with the rhythm concerned and, for each rhythm, with the individual.

For animals the synchronising factor is the alternation of light and darkness, while for human beings it is the alternation of the social habits of daytime activity and of sleep at night. As to the social habits, it used to be thought that they could be summed up in terms of work schedules and that, by working at night and sleeping in the daytime, the body could be gradually adapted to synchronisation with the occupational activity. It is now known, however, that the social factors of synchronisation are, in fact, of two kinds: on the one hand, those pertaining to the rhythm of work and, on the other, those pertaining to the rhythms of the family and of the community, which may be independent of the work rhythms and on which the organisation of time spent at work has little influence. It is necessary, therefore, to consider a model with three variables: the biological rhythm of the body, the rhythm of work, and the rhythm of the social and ecological environment.

Experimental research

In the circadian rhythms of plants and animals the synchronising factor is the alternation of light and darkness, changes in which are reflected in the rhythms. It has been found that, if the light/dark periods are inverted, the rhythms of plants,[1] mice,[2] etc., will be inverted as well. There must be no tampering, however, with the circadian rhythm's period of about 24 hours in the case of mammals: neuroses have been observed in monkeys subjected in laboratories to artifically created "days" of 12 or 48 hours.

Human beings, too, have been made the subject of experiments.

In conditions of complete isolation from all external synchronising factors, the biological rhythms retain very stable periods of about 24 hours. For example, the wakefulness/sleep cycle had an average duration of 24 hours and 31 minutes in an experiment involving a sojourn of several months in an underground cave.[3] Experiments carried out underground have also shown that, after the return to the surface and daylight, the process of re-synchronisation is completed in five days in the case of the body temperature but needs more than three weeks in the case of the 17-hydroxycorticosteroid rhythm in the urine.[4] The findings of these experiments refer to both the female and the male body.

In a laboratory isolated from the external world, manipulation of the factors of synchronisation (periodicity of lighting, specially adjusted clock, etc.) can create "artificial days" differing from the 24-hour day. When the time added or subtracted does not exceed a maximum of two hours, the rhythms become synchronised with the new time-scale. If, on the other hand, the

---

[1] Augustin de Candolle, quoted in Reinberg (1974), p. 33.

[2] Kalmus (1940).

[3] Siffre (1963).

[4] Reinberg et al. (1966), p. 262; Ghata et al. (1968), p. 269.

difference does exceed two hours, the process of re-synchronisation will be incomplete. For example, in the case of 30-hour "days", it has been found that the heartbeat, but not the body temperature, becomes re-synchronised,[1] while, in the case of 21-hour days obtained by using a specially adjusted watch in the Spitzbergen polar day, there was re-synchronisation of the urinary pH and of the excretion of sodium but not of potassium.[2]

This is a case of apparent or real de-synchronisation reflecting the simultaneous action of factors of synchronisation having different weights.[3] The rhythms thus have structures which vary with the rhythm and which are subject to the simultaneous influence of several different rhythms, including especially the rhythm of temperature and the rhythm of activity. As a result, there can be de-synchronisation, whether real or apparent and depending on the individual, between the various rhythms.

Transmeridian flights

Studies have been made also of long-distance flights.[4] North-south flights within the same time zone do not alter the pilot's biological rhythms. On the other hand, at the end of an east-west (or west-east) transmeridian flight, the pilot's biological rhythms, which are still synchronised with the local time at the airport of departure, will be in advance of (or will lag behind) the social and ecological rhythms of the place of landing. If the difference in clock time does not exceed five hours, the biological rhythms are not altered. If it does exceed five hours, it will take about a week for the biological rhythms to become adjusted to the place of arrival. Accordingly, pilots who have to make a return flight learn how to stay apart from the life around them at the end of their outward flight so as to retain the rhythms which they will find again at the end of their homeward flight.

Studies of night workers

None of the situations described above applies to night workers, who are exposed in the course of the nyctohemeral period to the discordance of two successive synchronising environments—that of their workplace and that of their place of residence.

When an investigation which lasted for 13 weeks of night work was concluded, it was noted that, when a worker changed from a day shift to a night shift, there was a narrowing of the amplitude of his biological rhythms [5] (though to an extent varying with the particular rhythm: the heartbeat, for example, being more labile than the body temperature), but that, as the maxima

---

[1] Gouars (1973).
[2] Simpson et al. (1970).
[3] Wever (1975).
[4] Lafontaine et al. (1967).
[5] Bonjer (1961).

remained diurnal,[1] there was no real inversion. It has nevertheless also been found that, during the first days after a phase-shifting from night work to daytime work, there is a marked de-synchronisation of the minima of the functions.

These variations are, moreover, also subject to the influence of extrinsic conditions, such as emotional stress, fatigue before beginning work, the nature of the task which is performed [2] and, especially, the fact that, on the weekly day of rest (when there are no occupational factors of synchronisation), the social and ecological factors of synchronisation re-establish the *status quo ante*.[3] Thus, in practice, there can never be any really continuous night work: there are always at least weekly rotations. That is why, even "if the worker is allowed time to adapt himself to the inversion of work and rest periods by working at night and sleeping by day over a period of several weeks except on Sundays, no real inversion occurs in the curve of nyctohemeral variations".[3]

For example, when the daily variations in body temperature of a man practising a normal schedule of wakefulness and sleep (work by day, rest at night) is compared with that of a man adopting an inverted schedule (work at night, sleep by day), it is found [4] that, despite the inversion of the schedules, the rhythm of the body temperature does not change.

Activation and de-activation; wakefulness and sleep

Every kind of behaviour, for whatever purpose, of the human body involves a measurable degree of mobilisation of energy which ranges from hypo-activation to hyperactivation, from slumber to a state of excitement. This behavioural activation depends on the activity of the central nervous system—that is, on the degree of wakefulness of the brain, which, in turn, is governed by two closely related parts of the brain: the reticular formation and the hypo-thalamus. The circadian variations in activation, or hyperwakefulness, and in de-activation, or hypowakefulness, and, in particular, the alternation of the awakened state and of sleep thus ultimately depend on the circadian variations in reticulo-hypothalamic activity.[5]

By means of the indicators of wakefulness, the alternations of the awakened state and of sleep can be noted and the varying degrees of activation which the awakened state and sleep comprise can be discerned.

In the case of the awakened state, electroencephalography can distinguish between attentive wakefulness (fast, low-voltage waves) and inattentive wakeful-ness (slower, high-voltage waves). Furthermore, psychometric tests can show

---

[1] In this study the term "diurnal", which sometimes means "daily", is used in the sense of "daytime".

[2] Tsaneva and Daleva (1975).

[3] Andlauer and Metz (1967), p. 279.

[4] Andlauer and Metz (1967).

[5] Moruzzi (1954); Magoun (1958).

that performance is at a maximum in the middle of the day and at its minimum after waking or before going to sleep.[1] The curves of variation in efficiency show a close correlation with the curves of the nyctohemeral rhythms of the autonomic function and especially with the variations in body temperature,[2] thereby clearly revealing the comprehensive psychosomatic nature of the circadian rhythms. It is to be noted, too, that there are faster rates of variation in efficiency corresponding to fluctuations in vigilance.[3]

In the case of sleep, electroencephalography reveals five stages ranging from light sleep (stages 1 and 2) to deep sleep (stages 3 and 4) with slow waves, followed by paradoxical sleep (stage 5) with rapid waves similar to the tracings of attentive wakefulness but with characteristic accompaniments: dreams, eye movements, disminished muscle tone. In the course of a single night's sleep, the stages are repeated several times in cycles of about 90 minutes, the paradoxical fifth stage, which is longer during the second half of the night, lasting for an average of ten minutes per cycle.

Changes in sleep

Man cannot survive lack of sleep for as long as he can survive deprivation of food. Experiments have shown that disorders brought on by lack of sleep soon occur: the loss of a single night's sleep causes on the following day a marked decline in the performance of various tests.[4] It has been found that a real state of stress develops when the deprivation of sleep is prolonged over three to five nyctohemeral periods, with deep metabolic disorders [5] and electro-cardiographic alteration in one-quarter of the subjects tested, a rise from 38 to 168 per cent in the rate of sedimentation in the blood, an increase of 19 per cent in protein-bound iodine and a fall of 26 per cent in serous iron.[6]

So far as the various stages of sleep are concerned, some research work has been done with a view to determining the stage of sleep that is indispensable for correcting the "damage" sustained during the awakened state. This question is, however, still unsettled. Some investigators give priority to the paradoxical stage; others, to the stage of deep sleep; while the most recent investigators [7] are of the opinion that it is not so much the duration of the various stages that should be considered as the total duration of sleep and the balanced succession of the cycles of alternating deep sleep and paradoxical sleep.

---

[1] Kleitman (1963).

[2] Loveland and Williams (1963).

[3] Bloch (1966).

[4] Metz et al. (1960), pp. 25-26.

[5] Kuhn (1967).

[6] Levi (1966).

[7] Johnson (1974). See also Agnew et al. (1966); Berger et al. (1962); Dement (1960); Jouvet (1962); Takahashi (1968); Hartmann (1970).

Work and fatigue

All the organs of the human body that relate man to his environment (muscles, central nervous system and sensory organs) are subject to fatigue: after working for some time at a certain level of intensity and of expenditure of energy (catabolism), they have to suspend activity temporarily in order to replenish their stores of energy (anabolism). It follows that work, which exemplifies man's relationship to his natural, technical and social environment, also produces fatigue and requires an alternation of exertion and rest.

Fatigue causes a particular proprioceptive sensation which indicates to the worker the strenuousness of his exertion and the limits beyond which he must not further exert himself. Fatigue thus acts as a behavioural regulator of activity. There can be no exertion, even voluntary or at play, without fatigue. Such fatigue is, however, physiological and not detrimental to health. On the other hand, if the worker disregards the warning sign of fatigue and goes on working, fatigue will not surrender so easily to rest and will build up as the days go by until, having become chronic, it will lead to pathological conditions of exhaustion or even of collapse, either organic (as in the case of the death of a competitor in a cycle race run in stages) or psychological (neuroses) or psychosomatic (stomach ulcers, myocardial infarctus, etc.).

Work activity sets up a complex hierarchical system of controls at three levels.

— At the highest level, whereas consciousness and deliberate activity are rooted in the cerebral cortex, it is the hypothalamus which, in association with the reticular formation, rules all unconscious regulation of work. The hypothalamus controls the mustering of energy required for the performance of work, causes the sensation of fatigue which halts that performance and controls the subsequent replenishment of energy reserves during rest. Being the organ of fatigue, whether normal or pathological,[1] the hypothalamus operates as the main regulator of work activity.

— At the endocrine level, the effects of work and of fatigue have been compared to those of stress as described by Hans Selye;[2] fatigue in such cases may be likened to a "minor post-aggressive response":[3] the hypothalamus, which in the body is next to the hypophisis, causes the secretion of an adenohypopheal hormone, or ACTH. This hormone acts in turn on the adrenal cortex, which, depending on the case, produces catabolic or anabolic hormones; the former (glucocorticoids) increase the 17-hydroxycorticocosteroids in the blood and, with a time-lag, in the urine, while the latter (protein-building) increase the 17-ketosteroids in the blood and in the urine.

— The third level, which affects directly the metabolisms in the energy and chemical composition of the tissues and cells, is that of the autonomous

---

[1] Chauchard (1962).

[2] Selye (1950).

[3] Bugard (1960), p. 61.

nervous system: the sympathetic system, whose mediators are adrenaline and noradrenaline, is ergotropic and catabolic, while the parasympathetic system, whose mediator is acetylcholin, is trophotrophic and anabolic. The rates of cathecholamines in the blood or urine are a fairly accurate indication of the activation of the sympathetic system and hence of the strenuousness of exertion.[1]

The signs of fatigue differ according to whether it is muscular or mental.

— In the case of physical work, the level of exertion is measured in relation to a zero point, which is taken as a condition of the muscles at rest; below a certain threshold of steady activity there is no sign of fatigue; above that threshold, the greater the exertion the sooner fatigue sets in; but pauses for rest during the day's work can correct it, at any rate to a large extent, and enable the worker to resume his activity.

— On the other hand, in the case of intellectual and mental work the level of exertion is measured in relation not to a zero point, which would be that of sleep, but to the average level of activation of the human body in the awakened state—a level which may be denoted as, say, level 2 in an arbitrary scale of activation. If the work activity corresponds exactly to that potential level of awakened activation—a level of "adequate average excitation", as it has been called [2]—there is no fatigue; fatigue appears only if the exertion required rises well above reference level 2 to level 3 (excess of fatigue) or falls well below it to level 1 (absence of fatigue). As for the correction of such fatigue, it takes place only on the following night after several hours of recuperative sleep.

Fatigue may be measured either subjectively by recourse to interviews and questionnaires or objectively by applying certain tests.

— Interviews and questionnaires provide information on fatigue experienced during and after work activity and also, in some cases, on accompanying disorders (asthenia, insomnia and character changes).

— The objective tests of fatigue generally measure not so much the fatigue itself, which is a residual condition, as the degree of strain which exertion puts directly on the body. In the absence of a comprehensive test of fatigue (tests proposed include the Donaggio reaction and the measurement of uropepsin), recourse is had to special indicators. In the case of physical exertion, the indicators are: intake of oxygen, heartbeat, corticosteroid and catecholamine rates in the urine, etc. In the case of mental fatigue, the indicators are: decline in work performance and in performance in psychometric tests; poor performance of a test task added to the occupational task (double-task method); diminution of sinus arrhythmia; flicker fusion threshold, which has to be interpreted with discrimination if central fatigue is not to be confused with peripheral visual fatigue; electroencephalographic

---

[1] von Euler (1953).
[2] Goldstein (1951), p. 96.

indications: trend towards de-activation in the tracings, modification of the aroused potentials by visual and auditory means.[1]

The main interest today is focused on methods that can be employed under actual working conditions: self-measurement,[2] double-task method, mobile electrophysiology laboratory for making telemetric recordings during work in the factory and during sleep at home.[3] It is always necessary, however, to provide also for tests of performance of tasks actually carried out because "the correlation between performance efficiency and body temperature, or subjective alertness, only holds for certain types of task".[4]

GENERAL PHYSIOLOGICAL AND PSYCHOLOGICAL EFFECTS

As was noted above, the circadian alternation of periods of wakefulness and sleep and of activity and rest is a biological phenomenon common to all higher animals and to man. Some animal species are diurnal, while others are nocturnal. Man has always belonged to the first category, and the fact that social and ecological factors of synchronisation have gradually taken the place of the atavistic light/darkness factors has not altered that basically diurnal nature of the human species.

As a result, the worker who has to work at night and sleep by day will suffer two forms of stress: stress in having to work during a period of de-activation, which will entail extra exertion; and stress in having to sleep during a period of activation, which raises the problem of sleep by day and of its restorative properties.

What this increased strain and diminished recuperation during sleep means for the night worker is additional fatigue, which will now be considered in its main aspects.

All the methods of measuring subclinical fatigue that were noted above have been employed for the purpose of revealing the specific fatigue inherent in night work, both regular and in rotating shifts.[5]

Effects on variations in physiological indicators

In the night worker, physiological indicators reveal the characteristic nocturnal decline, which is only slightly checked. The indicators concerned

---

[1] For a general description of the methods that have been proposed for the measurement of mental fatigue, see Schmidtke (1965), and Leplat and Schmidtke (1968), pp. 85-126. See also Kalsbeek (1965); Schmidtke (1951); Rey et al. (1974).

[2] Reinberg (1974), pp. 103-108.

[3] Mollet (1974); Pternitis (1975 a) and (1975 b).

[4] Folkard (1975).

[5] For a general exposition of the question, see Andlauer and Fourré (1962).

are heartbeat and blood pressure,[1] ventilation rate,[2] maximal aerobic power,[3] body temperature [4] and urinary excretion of corticosteroids [5] and catecholamines.[6]

The prevailing opinion is that, after a certain lapse of time (three to eight days), night work causes a narrowing in the amplitude of circadian variations of the biological indicators but that this tendency is corrected after a single day of rest during which sleep takes place at night,[7] as is the case with the weekly day of rest, so that (as was noted at the beginning of this chapter) there is no real inversion of the rhythms. Thus night work cannot benefit from the psychosomatic activation which facilitates work by day. It is therefore to be expected—and observation has confirmed—that, for an equal workload, night work will be more tiring than work in the daytime.

Effects on performance in psychological tests

It has been found that, among workers regularly employed on night work, there is an increase in motorial reaction time and a decline of performance in spoken word tests, with maxima at 3 a.m. concurrently with the fall in body temperature.[8] Similar results have been obtained [9] from the speed of response to an experimental test and from the level of the flicker fusion threshold. Again, faulty response in an experimental task is especially frequent between 4 and 6 a.m., when the speed of response and the detection of signals rate are hardly affected. Some observers have noted deterioration in the case of rotating shifts,[10] though not when recourse is had to the flicker fusion threshold and to the clock test.

Effects on sleep

As was shown above, sleep is characterised by its total duration, the duration of its various typical stages and the organisation or temporal structure of those stages.

A question that arises, therefore, is that of determining the characteristics of night workers' sleep by day.

---

[1] Menzel (1950); Burger et al. (1958); Solovieva and Gambashidze (1960); Barhad and Pafnote (1970).

[2] Burger et al. (1958).

[3] Ilmarinen et al. (1975).

[4] Bonjer (1961); Andlauer and Fourré (1965); Colquhoun et al. (1968).

[5] Reinberg (1974).

[6] Levi (1966); Tsaneva and Daleva (1975).

[7] Bonjer (1961).

[8] Solovieva and Gambashidze (1960).

[9] Kogi et al. (1975).

[10] Barhad and Pafnote (1970); Gavrilescu et al. (1966).

In the first place, its duration, whether measured by the questionnaire method [1] or directly by electroencephalographic recording,[2] has been found to be always shorter by one or two hours on the average than that of sleep by night.

This decrease in the average duration of sleep, which is already appreciable in the case of workers on the morning shift, is still more pronounced in the case of workers on the night shift. It has also been found that the later the worker goes to bed the shorter the duration of sleep, as if waking occurred at a more or less fixed hour whatever the time of going to bed. The duration of sleep is thus inversely proportional to the duration of the preceding state of wakefulness,[3] which is not in accordance with the hypothesis that "a debt of sleep" has been incurred but has been observed experimentally in the case of both animals [4] and human beings.[5] Apparently the spontaneous diurnal activation of the body causes premature awakening in both cases. Are there also external factors of synchronisation—light, noise of children, traffic noise, etc.—that cause the awakening? [6] They do not appear to be always a decisive cause.[7]

Sleep by day is not only of shorter duration but also more fragmented, since the rhythm of appetite for food interferes with the rhythm of sleep: it was found in one investigation that, in about one-third of the cases observed, sleep was interrupted at noon for a meal, which was then sometimes followed by a nap.

Sleep by day shows the same cyclical features as sleep by night.[7] In its brevity, it resembles the night sleep of short sleepers.[8] Daytime sleep cannot be likened, therefore, to total deprivation of sleep: there is always some "obligatory sleep" but there may not always be the "facultative sleep" which improves the quality of recuperation.[9] In that connection, studies of the question lay stress on the fact that sleep by day is less deep and more fitful,[10] as well as on the interruption of paradoxical sleep,[11] deep sleep being less affected. Early morning paradoxical sleep takes place sooner after sleep begins than in the night, but at the end

---

[1] Caillot (1959); Maurice and Monteil (1965); Quaas (1969); Tune (1969); Chazalette (1973); Guérin and Durrmeyer (1973).

[2] Lille (1967); Lille et al. (1968); Scherrer et al. (1968); Kripke et al. (1971); Forêt (1973); Mollet (1974); Ehrenstein and Müller-Limmroth (1975); Benoît (1976).

[3] Forêt (1973).

[4] Webb and Friedman (1969).

[5] Aschoff (1970).

[6] Thiis-Evenson (1958); Ehrenstein and Müller-Limmroth (1975); Knauth and Rutenfranz (1975).

[7] Lille (1967).

[8] Webb and Agnew (1970); Hartmann et al. (1971).

[9] Baekeland and Hartmann (1970).

[10] Gabersek et al. (1965); Mollet (1974).

[11] Forêt (1973); Pternitis (1975 a).

of the morning it is then, as it were, swept away by the rising circadian activation.[1] It is this diminution of paradoxical sleep that may cause the sensation of malaise commonly experienced by night workers on awakening.[2]

Effects on fatigue

Night workers are subject to over-fatigue, which appears to be due to the fact that they have to work in a state of nocturnal de-activation and to sleep in a state of diurnal re-activation. Over-fatigue is thus caused by a discordance of phase between two circadian rhythms—the biological rhythm of the body's activation and psychosomatic de-activation, and the artificial rhythm of activity at work and rest. This fact has been well established in an objective test of mental fatigue (average aroused visual potential) showing that the fatigue of shift workers varies not only with the workload but also, for an equal workload, with the shift: there is less fatigue in the afternoon, owing to the activation of the body and to the quality of the preceding nocturnal sleep.[3]

These theoretical concepts and experimental findings are indirectly confirmed by findings, to be described below, relating to variations in criteria of occupational activity such as output, safety and absenteeism.

EFFECTS ON SOME CRITERIA OF OCCUPATIONAL ACTIVITY

Effects on output

The output of rotating shifts is generally thought to be lower at night than by day.[4] If that is so, what is the cause of that diminution in output? Is it due to the over-fatigue [5] of night work or only to a lessened pressure on workers to produce when they are on the night shift? The results of several studies lend support to the first explanation. Thus, in a study of teleprinters working on rotating shifts, records were made of the number of calls and of the intervals of time between the calls and the operators' replies. For each of the three shifts there was the same supervision; yet the level of performance on the night shift, when there were fewer calls than during the two other shifts, was found to be by far the lowest.[6] In another study, about 175,000 entries of meter readings and other figures made in the ledger of a gasworks from 1912 to 1931 were examined. It was found that proneness to error was at its height during the night, reaching a high peak level at 3 a.m.—that is, at the hour when circadian de-activation is most pronounced.[7] Falls of, respectively, 20

---

[1] Forêt (1973).
[2] Hartmann et al. (1971).
[3] Pternitis (1969), (1972) and (1975 b).
[4] Wyatt and Marriott (1953).
[5] Kogi and Saito (1971).
[6] Browne (1955).
[7] Bjerner et al. (1955).

and 5 per cent have been found in the outputs of rotating night shifts in a sugar refinery and in a wire-works. In both cases the output of the night shift, like the body temperature of the workers, rose continuously from the Monday to the Saturday.[1] Yet another study has shown that, in the case of long cycles of rotating shifts, lowered output at night is particularly pronounced during the second week of night work. It does seem, therefore, that the decline in output that has been found among night workers is attributable to their circadian de-activation and to their consequent additional fatigue.

A study carried out from another angle in Algeria [2] has shown a fall in productivity with the introduction of the system (also applied in some German undertakings) of two long rotating shifts of 11 and 13 hours. There were frequent and longer pauses from work and there was more absenteeism. The study also notes cases of nervous, cardiac and digestive disorders.

Again, it has been found in a railway investigation that "the daily course of the relative frequency of automatically induced emergency brakes as well as the daily course of the hourly frequency of acoustical warning signals of the safety device, both caused by errors of omission of engine drivers...., exhibited a double peaked curve, one of them occurring in the night around 3 a.m." (as in the case of the reading of gas meter records referred to above), while the other occurred "around 3 p.m. in the early afternoon".[3] These findings show one effect of fatigue on vigilance.

Effects on safety

Similar results relating to the seriousness of industrial accidents have been obtained from an analysis of the times at which 11,000 accidents occurred in a group of metallurgical and mining industries.[4] This study shows that the rate of *serious* accidents occurring during the night shift is higher than the rate over the whole period of 24 hours and that the accident rate is lower than the average during the night shift and higher than the average during the morning shift. The proneness of night workers to serious accidents has been attributed to the decline of higher brain activity at night.[5] Studies of the accident rate have produced somewhat varied findings. Some investigators have found a significantly high accident rate at the beginning of the night shift.[6] Others have found that the accident rate does not rise significantly during the night shift.[5] It has been reported, for example, that the majority of accidents in three pits of the Pecs-Mecsek coal basin in Hungary occurred during the afternoon shift, which is generally held to be the least fatiguing.[7]

---

[1] Meers (1974).

[2] Mokrane (1971).

[3] Hildebrandt et al. (1975).

[4] J. Kubler, quoted in Andlauer and Metz (1967).

[5] Andlauer and Fourré (1962).

[6] Farmer and Chambers, quoted in Surry (1971).

[7] Köhegyi and Bédi (1962).

In the case of a drilling operation in the Sahara which was continuous (so that the distribution of the schedules of the various jobs played no role), it was found that the accident rate was affected not by the schedules but by climatic conditions: there was a definite improvement in the rate during the night and in winter-time, when temperatures were lower.[1]

Effects on absenteeism

It is well known that the factors accounting for absenteeism are many and varied. It is therefore difficult to relate that broad indicator to a specific cause of fatigue in night work. In the case of rotating shifts, the rate of absenteeism has been found to be higher in the night shift. When shift rotation is at intervals longer than one week, absenteeism in the night shift has been found to increase in proportion to the duration of night work. Other studies have, however, produced opposite results.[2] Thus convincing evidence is lacking—so much so that, where the rate of absenteeism of regular daytime shifts has been found to be higher (by as much as 30 per cent in one case [3]) in a regular daytime shift than in rotating shifts with night work,[4] the difference vanishes if the workers in the regular daytime shift who had been moved to that shift from rotating shifts (usually for health reasons) are excluded from the calculation.

MEDICAL AND PATHOLOGICAL EFFECTS

It has long been known that there are chronosemeiological phenomena: illnesses often show a cyclical periodicity, such as the monthly periodicity of the mental disorder of "lunatics" or the circadian periodicity of allergies or the attacks of gout at cock-crow, etc. It has, however, also been shown that there is a chronopathology [5] in which the time factor does not only affect the form of the disorders but also contributes to their generation: a dose of an endotoxin "compatible with survival for most animals at one time is highly lethal when injected into comparable mice in a different stage of rhythm". There seems to be a link here with the over-fatigue of night workers in that it marks the aggression of a strain (work) at a time (night) of least resistance.

It would have been useful at this stage to distinguish between what, in this pathology, pertains to night work as such and what pertains to the rotation of shifts. As the inadequacy of studies of regular night work stands in the way of that distinction, it is the combined effect of the two aggressions, which are in any case usually associated in industrial work, that will be considered.

---

[1] Mouton (1960).

[2] Hogg (1961).

[3] Aanonsen (1959).

[4] Thiis-Evensen (1958).

[5] Halberg (1960).

General morbidity

In 1959 the Medical Inspector of Factories for the Municipality of Oslo published the results of a comparative study of the health of day workers and shift workers which he had made while acting as physician to two electro-metallurgical factories and one electrochemical factory during the six-year period from 1948 to 1954.[1] The results include the percentage frequencies (see table, p. 28) of various psychosomatic disorders among 345 day workers who had never been shift workers; 380 shift workers, some of whom had never been day workers while the remainder had been day workers for only short periods; and 128 day workers who had been transferred from shift work to daytime work for medical reasons.

These statistics are of particular interest in that they show that the transfer, whether spontaneous or on medical advice, of workers in poor health from rotating shifts to regular daytime shifts can conceal a high rate of morbidity in rotating shifts. From the epidemiological point of view this point is of particular interest: it means that little reliance can be attached to the results of investigations which neglect to take account of such transfers of workers.

Apart from digestive and nervous disorders, the rate of morbidity has been found to be much the same [2] among daytime workers as among workers on rotating shifts and even lower among the latter by reason of the fact that they have been selected.[3] In particular, shift workers are not subject to specific cardiovascular morbidity, although coronary affections have often been regarded as symptoms of fatigue, especially at the level of foremen. This applies also to regular night work, which does not appear to have had any bearing on the incidence of myocardial infarction found in hospital staff.[4] It is to be noted, however, that cases of rheumatic arthritis have been found more frequently among rotating shift workers than among other workers.[5]

Digestive disorders

Night workers' meals

Regular night work disrupts the circadian rhythm of nutrition. As a rule, but depending on local practice, it involves a meal during the night—that is, during a period of digestive de-activation—with the two main diurnal meals (of which the one taken in the middle of the day may interrupt sleep) being maintained; the night meal, usually cold, is eaten without any appetite [6] and is apt to be seasoned with condiments and taken with stimulants (coffee, alcohol);[7]

---

[1] Aanonsen (1959); see also Thiis-Evensen (1958).

[2] Smith and Vernon (1928); Hesselgreen et al. (1948).

[3] Brusgaard (1949); Leuliet (1963).

[4] Chevrolle (1963).

[5] Mott et al. (1965).

[6] Wyatt and Marriott (1953).

[7] Dervillée and Lazarini (1959).

Class of disorder	345 day workers	380 shift workers	128 former shift workers
Gastric	7.5	6.0	19.0
Digestive	17.0	20.2 [1]	32.5
Nervous	13.0	10.0	32.5
Cardiac	2.6	1.1	0.8

[1] Estimated.

eating three meals instead of the usual two can overwork the digestive system [1] and can lead to obesity (as was found in a study of female nurses on night duty in the case of 20 per cent of them [2]).

For these disorders that are due to regular night work the rotation of work schedules is not a lasting remedy but merely introduces a further pathogenic factor, that is, the irregularity of meals. Thus it seems that unrhythmic nutrition is at the root of the pronounced digestive disorders [3] that will now be described and which have in fact been observed among workers on rotating shifts.

Gastric and intestinal disorders

Apart from ulcers, which will be referred to below, the digestive disorders to be considered here are of so many kinds that they cannot be examined in detail: their only common characteristic is that they are statistically correlated with rotating work schedules.

Dyspeptic disorders (hyperesthenic dyspepsia of rotating work schedules,[4] hyposthenic dyspepsia [3]) are mentioned in a study which found two or three times more cases of non-ulcerous gastric disorders among shift workers than among daytime workers.[5]

With regard to intestinal disorders, constipation, which is sometimes associated with haemorrhoidal affections, may form part of the "syndrome of the week of night work".[6]

Gastric and duodenal ulcers

Digestive ulcers identified by X-ray are more common among workers on rotating shifts than among those who work regularly by day. It is to be noted, however, that, according to the results of a rather brief three-year study of

---

[1] Hogg (1961).
[2] Laplanche and Brault (1963).
[3] Dervillée and Lazarini (1959).
[4] Gaultier et al. (1961).
[5] Andersen (1958).
[6] Lecocq (1963); Mott et al. (1965).

workers on rotating shifts carried out in an oil refinery which took into account the transfer of workers from rotating shifts to daytime work, no abnormal incidence of digestive ulcers was found among the workers on rotating shifts.[1]

Gastroduodenal ulcers are a typical form of psychosomatic disorder. In that connection, it is no longer possible to accept the formerly held classic view that irregular meals and faulty diets lead first to functional and then to organic disorders of the digestive system. It is now known that ulcers are a common somatic manifestation of a dysfunction of the central nervous system and particularly of the hypothalamus, which is the organ of fatigue. Pylonic and duodenal ulcers have been produced in animals simply by prolonged stimulation in the hypothalamus.[2] In an experiment on a tethered or otherwise immobilised rat it was found that it developed an ulcer only if its sleep was disturbed in such a way that it was deprived of deep sleep or of paradoxical sleep.[3] Reference must be made at this point to the deep hypothalamic disturbances caused by the conflict between organic and occupational rhythms, which points to a common pathogeny forming a bridge between digestive syndromes and neurotic syndromes and explains the statistical link between them.

Nervous disorders

Frequency

Over-fatigue due to the regular or rotating performance of night work causes an increase in nervous morbidity which has been statistically established, even though the nosology of the disorders considered in investigations is in many cases inadequately described. It has been found, for example, that there are two-and-a-half times (64 per cent) more nervous disorders among workers on rotating shifts than among day workers (25 per cent)[4] and that, as was indicated above, 32 per cent of the workers formerly on rotating shifts who were moved to day shifts suffered from nervous disorders as against only 13 per cent of the workers who had always been employed on normal schedules.[5] The essential pathogenic factor here is not the rotating nature of the work schedules but the night work itself, as has been shown in a study which found that 45 per cent of the workers on regular night shifts were affected as against 36 per cent of the workers on rotating shifts.[6]

Pathogeny

It was noted above that the cause of the over-fatigue of the night worker is twofold: on the one hand, his work is performed during a period of nocturnal

[1] Demaret and Fialaire (1974).

[2] French et al. (1954).

[3] Cosnier, quoted in Bugard (1974), Vol. 2, p. 72.

[4] Andersen (1958).

[5] Aanonsen (1959).

[6] Uhlich (1957).

de-activation and is, therefore, more fatiguing; on the other hand, his sleep takes place during a period of diurnal activation and is, therefore, less restorative. These are also the two sources of the night worker's neurosis.

The first factor brings up the well known notion of occupational over-exertion. It has been found, for example, that an excessive intellectual or mental workload causes neuroses among telephonists,[1] telegraphists [2] and office machinery operators.[3] In the case, however, of night workers, over-exertion occurs not so much because the workload is excessive as because the de-activation of the body reduces its capacity to cope with the workload; the strain becomes pathogenic, not because of an increase in stress, but because of the nocturnal asthenia of those organs of the body that relate man to the external world.

It is, however, the disturbance of sleep by day which is the more important factor. In the first place, sleeping disorders are extremely frequent among night workers. For example, they have been found in one investigation among 60 per cent of rotating shift workers as against 11 per cent of day workers;[4] in another investigation, among 66 and 11 per cent, respectively, of these two categories of workers;[5] and, in yet another investigation, among 50 to 62 per cent of night workers, whether or not on rotating shifts, as against only 5.2 per cent of day workers.[6] The rate of incidence of sleep disorders increases among rotating shift workers in proportion to the duration of night work.[7] In a study of a group of former rotating shift workers moved to the day shift, it was found that 84 to 97 per cent of them had suffered sleep disorders when they worked at night.[8]

Secondly, these sleeping disorders appear at an early stage prior to the other forms of neuroses so that, between the stage of simple fatigue of the night worker and the appearance of a pronounced neurotic syndrome, there is a separable intermediate and pre-neurotic stage appearing only as a deep disturbance of sleep.

Lastly, and especially, sleeping problems appear nowadays to be a symptom (or even, some would say, the cause) of a more basic metabolic disorder.[9] The two main stages of sleep to which reference has already been made—the stage of deep sleep and the stage of paradoxical sleep—being marked by secretions of, respectively, anabolic and catabolic hormones,[10] it is the balance

---

[1] Begoin (1958).
[2] Ferguson (1973).
[3] Grandjean (1969).
[4] Thiis-Evenson (1958).
[5] Andersen (1958).
[6] Uhlich (1957).
[7] Burger et al. (1958).
[8] Aanonsen (1959).
[9] Bugard (1974), Vol. 2, p. 152.
[10] Takahashi (1968).

between deep sleep and paradoxical sleep which regulates the metabolic balance between anabolism and catabolism. It has been found, however, that the due proportions of deep sleep and paradoxical sleep are disorganised in the sleep of the average depressed worker.[1] Correlative studies show that the hypothalamic and corticoadrenal secretions are also disorganised.[2] On the other hand, anti-depressant medication simultaneously brings about a gradual regularisation of the cycles of sleep and of the hormonal rhythms with a concomitant improvement of the symptoms. This has led one observer to regard mental depression as a "malady of the rhythms" and a "pathology of circadianism",[3] which, surely, is just what the night worker's neurosis mainly is. In his case, it is the disorganisation of the rhythms due to the work schedule that is the cause of the depression.

Night worker's neurosis

The night worker's neurosis is one of the "situational pseudo-neuroses",[4] which is an appellation clearly indicating that it is due to working conditions (that is, in the night worker's case, the performance of night work) and not to any prior endogenous conflict, although certain personality traits may influence the form that it takes. This neurosis does not differ clinically from other occupational neuroses. Its symptoms are the usual three: general weakness, especially in the morning, insomnia with subsequent sleepiness and character disorders of the aggressive or depressive type.[5] Its development varies. It may appear during the first few months of night work [6] and it may either lessen as the worker becomes used to it or require his transfer to a day shift, which will cause it to disappear. In other cases, it appears only after 10 or 20 years of night work, probably in conjunction with the effects of age. In such cases it requires a change of employment, which, however, may not always suffice to make it disappear.

Drugs

It was noted above that night work could lead to wrong diets and to the use of alcoholic beverages. It can also lead to the taking of too many drugs to sleep by day and to keep awake at night and then to more and more drugs with the onset of sleep disorders and of the disorders of an incipient neurosis. A vicious circle is then created: "fatigue, insomnia, taking of hypnotic drugs, protection against loss of vigilance, increased hypnogenic doses, greater fatigue on waking, taking of stimulants before going to work".[7] The number of night workers who take psychotropic drugs, though not accurately known, must be

---

[1] Zung (1965).

[2] Sachar et al. (1971); Sachar et al. (1973).

[3] Bugard (1964).

[4] ibid., p. 50.

[5] Begoin (1958).

[6] Andersen (1958).

[7] Held (1967).

considerable according to international statistics relating to road safety,[1] which show that 20 to 30 per cent of drivers take such drugs. These drugs cause poor performance in tests, especially when they are taken after loss of sleep or in conjunction with alcohol.[2] It may be readily supposed that these behavioural disturbances can give rise to industrial and traffic accidents.

Conclusions

Thus it has appeared that night work, whether regular or in rotating shifts, can cause permanent damage to the hypothalamus, leading to a psychosomatic illness in the form of either a neurotic syndrome or an ulcerous type of digestive syndrome. Night work performed in rotating shifts may give rise, furthermore, to digestive disorders liable to develop on their own or in conjunction with psychosomatic illness.

Epidemiological studies have established, in both cases, that the ailments are occupational in origin.

EFFECTS OF THE CHARACTER OF THE TASK ON REACTIONS TO NIGHT WORK

For more than a century workers seem to have stood up fairly well to shift work, traditionally practised in continuously operating factories, mining, etc. That is no longer the case today, especially in the mechanised and automated jobs of the technologically advanced industries. It is as if technical progress had aggravated the problem, as indeed it has. An investigation covering more than 500 workers, relating their jobs to their tolerance of alternating night work, shows that tolerance (measured by physiological indicators, psychological tests and interviews) diminishes with the diminution of the physical load (heavy work, hot atmosphere) and its replacement with an intellectual and mental workload (supervisory work and its accompanying responsibilities).[3]

A reported case of a very severely affected group is that of workers in a continuously operating refinery on shifts with weekly rotation (sleep disorders, 89 per cent; nervous disorders, 50 per cent; digestive disorders, 47 per cent, of which 25 per cent were cases of chronic gastritis or ulcers); for the same type of activity but with a mainly mental workload, the disturbances are less pronounced in the case of semi-continuous work (that is, with Sunday rest), as well as in the case of continuous shifts with short rotations (every other day).[4] Yet even in the last two cases, adaptation is much poorer than has been found among workers with a mixed physical and mental workload and especially among labourers. That the character of the task which is performed has an effect has been confirmed in other studies.[5]

---

[1] Crespy (1974).
[2] Pternitis (1975 a).
[3] Barhad and Pafnote (1970).
[4] Meers (1974); Guérin and Durrmeyer (1973).
[5] Tsaneva and Daleva (1975).

These facts can be interpreted by reference to what, in connection with the pathogeny of nervous disorders, was noted above on the restorative properties of, respectively, deep sleep and paradoxical sleep. Deep sleep is preeminently the anabolic stage of sleep which replenishes the stores of energy and corrects the fatigue of the muscles; in fact, physical exercise prolongs its duration in the following period of sleep.[1] Sleep by day does not appreciably disturb that stage of sleep.[2]

Paradoxical sleep has an entirely different significance: it is active, produces dreams and is catabolic (being accompanied by peak levels of 17-hydroxy-corticosteroid secretions in plasma).[3] It appears to play a specific role in the correction of mental fatigue, since intellectual exertion increases the following paradoxical sleep [2] while its suppression in experiments leads to neurosis.[4] This dreaming activity—"this irrational but necessary proliferation of the subconscious"—must be preserved, therefore, "in order to ensure the mental equilibrium of the individual".[5] Yet in sleep by day, the paradoxical stage is severely curtailed.[6]

It is thus possible to settle the controversy—referred to above with regard to the physiological changes occurring in sleep by day—concerning the respective values of deep sleep and paradoxical sleep. Both of them are restorative but the former corrects physical fatigue while the latter corrects mental fatigue. Sleep by day retains a sufficient amount of deep sleep to correct the nocturnal fatigue of the labourer but not enough dreaming to correct mental overwork.

The character of the task plays an important role: the labourer stands up to night work better than the worker whose activity is mainly mental for the simple reason that sleep by day, which comprises much deep sleep, can replenish the stores of energy and correct physical fatigue whereas it cannot correct mental fatigue owing to the curtailment of indispensable paradoxical sleep. Since technical advances tend to replace physically arduous jobs by preponderantly mental jobs, it must be presumed that the harm is bound to be aggravated in the future with the growth of mechanisation and automation.

EFFECTS OF SOME INDIVIDUAL CHARACTERISTICS OF WORKERS

The effects that will now be successively considered are, first, those of age and length of service; next, those of proneness to emotion and of character factors; and lastly, those of sex, with consideration also of the pathology of female employment.

---

[1] Baekeland and Lasky (1966).

[2] Forêt (1973).

[3] Weitzman et al. (1966).

[4] Jouvet (1962).

[5] Bugard (1974), Vol. 2, p. 179.

[6] Forêt (1973); but Johnson (1974) would blame rather the disturbance of the deep sleep/paradoxal sleep cycles, though the argument would be the same.

Effects of ageing and seniority

As has been shown, the over-fatigue and the specific pathology of night workers result from two causes: exertion during nocturnal de-activation, and insufficiently restorative sleep during diurnal activation. Ageing aggravates both factors: psychological and physiological decline further increase occupational strain, and the disturbances of sleep due to ageing reduce still further its restorative properties. The first effect is well known. With advancing age the composition of nocturnal sleep undergoes a change in both sexes. After the age of 40 awakenings are more frequent,[1] and deep sleep diminishes constantly from birth to death while paradoxical sleep remains at its peak level until an advanced age.[2] To these general declines daytime sleep adds particular alterations, including especially the curtailment of paradoxical sleep referred to above. The daytime sleep of the ageing night worker thus loses its restorative properties. The deficit in the pre-eminently anabolic deep sleep accentuates the insufficiency of restoration of the tissues which characterises senescence, while the curtailment of paradoxical sleep (which, as has already been noted, affects adult night workers) promotes a transition to chronic occupational mental fatigue. This complementary character of the effects of ageing and of night work has led some to consider that overwork due to night work constitutes "functional" ageing,[3] to be distinguished from chronological ageing.

The foregoing discussion finds confirmation in several investigations. One of them [4] covers 105 workers falling into three age groups: under 25, 25 to 39 and 40 and over. Sleep was found to be disturbed in 15 per cent of the workers in the first group, 52 per cent in the second and 71.7 per cent in the third. Definite pathological disorders were not found in the first group but affected 18.5 per cent of the workers in the second group and 21.8 per cent of those in the third. Another investigation, which covered 1,076 steel workers on rotating work schedules,[5] found that the incidence of sleep disorders increased significantly with length of service, age alone not being decisive. The same increase in the incidence of pathological disorders was found in an investigation covering 1,059 shift workers.[6] The conclusion to which these findings point is that, with the passage of years, there is no habituation to night work but rather growing intolerance of it.

These unfavourable results become all the more so when account is taken of the turnover of workers on shifts, which, as was shown in an early study referred to previously, is always considerable.[7] Other studies of this question

---

[1] Williams et al. (1974).

[2] Feinberg (1969); Forêt (1973).

[3] Ostberg and Svensson (1975).

[4] Chazalette (1973).

[5] Guérin and Devèze (1974).

[6] Andlauer and Fourré (1965).

[7] Aanonsen (1959).

may be mentioned. The results of one of them show that, in the course of the month following the assignment of workers to night work, from 10 to 15 per cent of them—7 per cent of those aged under 25, according to another study [1]—are soon obliged by digestive disorders to leave night work. The selected workers who do not have to leave night work are found to be appreciably more satisfied than workers with a shorter length of service with rotating work schedules.[2] Nevertheless, as the years go by, an increasing number of such workers also become subject in their turn to the "syndrome of night work" and are obliged to abandon night work towards the age of 50.[3] The results of yet another study show that only 40 per cent of workers on rotating shifts spend the whole of their working life on shifts.[4]

The age factor also operates in another way: the older the worker is when he starts on night work, the more slowly does he become adapted to it. Most of the writers on this question advise, therefore, that workers aged over 40 [1] or 50 [3] should not be recruited for night work.

Possible effects of other individual characteristics

For equal workloads, resistance to night work varies with the individual worker, as was shown in the statistics of morbidity given above. As age and sex do not suffice to explain this difference between one worker and another, physiological and psychological factors, which will now be considered, may account for it.

Physiological factors

Some writers confirm the prevailing opinion that there are "evening people" and "morning people", which suggests that both the former and the latter should be assigned to the regular shift that best suits them. When the incidence of age on the circadian variation of the heartbeat is studied, it is found that activation of the body occurs mainly in the morning among young people and mainly in the evening among older people. The nyctohemeral rhythm of excretion of adrenaline varies according to whether the individual is in better form in the morning or in the evening.[5] It may be that this morning/evening dichotomy is related to the bimodal nature of sleep at night:[6] deep sleep appears to occur in two stages, one of them between bedtime and 2 a.m., and the other towards 4 or 5 a.m. This might suggest that morning people make use of especially the first stage and evening people, the second. It must be admitted,

---

[1] Buffet (1963).
[2] Mann and Hoffmann (1960).
[3] Thiis-Evensen (1958).
[4] Leuliet (1963).
[5] Pátkai (1971).
[6] Viaud (1947).

however, that the concentration of the indispensable paradoxical sleep on the closing period of the night does not bear out that hypothesis.

Other writers have been concerned with variations in the lability of the circadian rhythms as affected by night work. Some of them [1] consider that genetic peculiarities of the individual are involved, which might be revealed in experimental tests and serve for the selection of night workers. Yet how could such tests be made when it is not yet known whether one should try to adapt the rhythms to the work schedules?

Psychosomatic factors

The psychosomatic nature of the night workers' syndrome points to an inquiry into its possible relations with the psychological peculiarities of individuals. Accordingly, consideration will be given here successively to proneness to emotion, character typology and states of depression.

Emotion increases the strain caused by a situation of stress. That strain is no doubt a function of the intensity [2] and of the quality [3] of the stimulus, but those who are prone to emotion react more than placid persons to a given experimental stimulus: their plasma cortisol is significantly higher.[4] A similar difference has been found in the secretion of ACTH among hospital patients about to undergo serious operations.[5]

A character typology distinguishes between an obsessive type, who bottles up his emotions, an hysterical type, who exteriorises them, and a balanced average type.[6] The three types of character react differently to an emotional impact. The differences do not reflect, however, unequal vulnerability to the impact: in particular, the excretions of catecholamines are identical in the three cases.[7] On the other hand, peculiarities of character affect the efficiency of persons assigned to experimental work, depending on what that work involves: the obsessional type works more precisely, the hysterical type more rapidly, and so on. Such peculiarities might be of aid, therefore, in predicting occupational adaptability.[8]

It is, however, only in passing that proneness to emotion and character have been mentioned, mainly because they can have only an indirect bearing—through the intermediary of a variation in the level of strain—on the disorders affecting night workers. Tendencies to depression are, on the other hand, another matter.

---

[1] For example, Mouret (1974).

[2] Frankenhaueser et al. (1962); Frankenhaueser et al. (1965/66).

[3] Levi (1965); Pátkai (1971).

[4] Raab (1968).

[5] Mason et al. (1965).

[6] Bugard (1974), Vol. 2, p. 75.

[7] Frankenhaueser et al. (1962); Frankenhaueser and Pátkai (1965); Levi (1965); Caille (1966).

[8] Caille et al. (1968).

Depression forms an integral part of the night worker's neurotic syndrome. The question to be considered is not, therefore, that of an *a posteriori* identification of depression but of the particular vulnerability to which a prior tendency to depression might expose a night worker. There are some facts that tend to bear out the hypothesis that workers who are apparently in good health but are inclined to depression react less well to an experimental stress than more dynamic workers: they mobilise poorly their sympathetico-adrenal system and their secretion of adrenaline and noradrenaline is smaller.[1] In an investigation carried out in the field, 15 workers well adapted to their work were compared with 15 ill adapted workers;[2] most of the former (14 out of 15) were energetic and dynamic, while most of the latter were depressed (13 out of 15) and frustrated since childhood (12 out of 15). Furthermore, most of the writers who have investigated the disorders of night workers have been led to suspect, in a number of affected workers, the existence of an early neurotic abnormality which made them more susceptible to the aggression of the work schedules.[3] This correlation is not, however, close enough—nor is the prior diagnosis sufficiently precise—for that supposition to serve the purpose of devising methods of selection.

Effects of sex

Women's night work

Night work for women is generally banned; it is tolerated in only a small number of occupations, is regarded as exceptional and has received little attention from investigators. The discussion here will therefore be mainly by analogy and hypothetical, with a view to determining whether there are certain psychological, physical and medical peculiarities which characterise women in relation to night work.

From a physiological point of view, a first point to be noted is that certain indicators subject to circadian variation differ in absolute terms between men and women. For example, the heartbeat is faster and the basic metabolism is lower in women than in men; but that in no way alters the curve of the nyctohemeral variation itself and therefore has no particular bearing on night work. On the other hand, interference of the 24-hour circadian rhythms with the 28-day ovarian cycle, causing the physiological indicators to express the product of the combined action of the nyctohemeral period and of the lunar month, means that some diurnal activation is intensified on some days of the month and that, on other days, nocturnal de-activation is more pronounced. Women thus have a specific "temporal structure",[4] as has been confirmed experimentally, particularly on the occasion when a woman remained in

---

[1] Roessler and Greenfield (1962); Frankenhaueser and Pátkai (1965).

[2] Van Alphen de Veer (1955).

[3] Burger et al. (1958); Andersen (1958); Thiis-Evensen (1958).

[4] Reinberg and Ghata (1964), pp. 57-64; Reinberg (1974), p. 59.

isolation for three months in an underground cave.[1] That specific structure, which is a function of the ovarian secretion, appears at the age of puberty and lasts throughout the period of genital activity, which is the main period of a woman's working life, and disappears with the menopause; after the age of about 50, the hormonal secretions and their gradual decline under the effect of senescence are alike in men and women.[2] In the course of the month the interference in question may affect the woman's resistance to certain forms of aggression, as, for example, her cutaneous susceptibility to heat[3] or her cutaneous reaction to histamine, the monthly variation of which disappears if the woman uses contraceptives which eliminates menstruation.[4]

It seems that this concept of "time of diminished resistance"[5] can be extended to the particular stress which is work; it would explain the monthly variations in the output of women workers (e.g. office machinery operators)[6] which has been noted by various writers, the pre-menopausal fatigue of women employees,[7] etc. As for night work, it is thought to expose women to fatigue on certain days of the ovarian cycle because their nocturnal de-activation is then greater than that of men—a fatigue that could have long-term effects bordering on the pathological. Two instances may be given.[8] In air hostesses exposed to the disturbances of the transmeridian flight schedules, there is, after a while, an increase in the production of male hormones, whereas the androgynous hormones of the pilots diminish so that the hormonal secretions of the two sexes tend to become uniform. The considerable increase of corticosteroids in the blood and the secondary obesity which hospital night duty can cause in the case of female nurses have not been found in the case of the male staff.[9] One conclusion that has been reached is that "women appear to have a method of adapting generally to odd working hours which is different from that of men".[8] This difference between the sexes, which would have to be confirmed by other studies, is worth mentioning but does not really constitute a counter-indication for night work for women.

Pathology of women night workers

Little study has been made of the pathology of women night workers— apart from a comparative study of an eight-hour three-shift system with a

---

[1] Reinberg et al. (1966); Ghata et al. (1968).

[2] Pincus (1947); Pincus et al. (1954).

[3] Procacci, quoted in Reinberg (1974), p. 71.

[4] Smolensky et al. (1974).

[5] Halberg (1960).

[6] Bugard (1974), Vol. 2, p. 90.

[7] Ginesta (1974).

[8] Bugard (1964).

[9] The obesity of hospital night staff might be due, therefore, to two causes: overloading of the digestive system, to which reference has already been made and which can affect both sexes, and an endocrine disorder which specifically affects the female staff.

system including 12-hour or 16-hour night shifts for female nurses in a Japanese hospital,[1] which shows that, while long shifts with more off-days do have some advantages, their effects on fatigue must not be underrated and that "important factors for evaluating night shift length would be workload patterns, evening work, rest allowances and social backgrounds".

Arguing, however, by analogy, it can be considered that women are not more subject than men to the digestive and nervous disorders caused by night work. Indeed, it has been found that digestive disorders occur more frequently among men than among women, ulcers being four times more frequent. Mental disorders show a similar sex difference. According to a United States census of mental patients who had been first admitted to hospital between 1922 and 1945, the proportion of women was systematically smaller—by about one-quarter—than the proportion of men.[2] An inquiry covering 3,000 workers in light industry in Britain which was carried out between 1942 and 1944 showed, it is true, that serious neuroses affected 9.1 per cent of the male workers as against 11 per cent of the female workers and that 19.2 per cent of the male workers, as against 23 per cent of the female workers,[3] were suffering from minor neurotic disorders. Since then, however, it has been generally recognised that the higher proportion of neuroses that has sometimes been found among women workers is due, not to their sex, but to the fact that their occupations, the intellectual and mental characteristics of feminine occupations (telephone operators, office machinery operators, regulated assembly-line work, etc.) are, on the average, more conducive to neurosis than the heavier work done by men. For example, an investigation covering mixed groups of telephone operators and of railway sorting-office employees has shown that the incidence of neurotic disorders is the same among men as among women.[4]

The conclusion that emerges is thus that, apart from the counter-indications already mentioned, there is no general physiological or medical counter-indication for women's night work.

Nevertheless, as has been pointed out in an ILO report:[5]

The main purpose of many of the regulations relating specifically to women's work is to protect their function of reproduction and it is protection of maternity that has been, in many cases, the legislator's prime concern. In strictly limiting the duration of women's work, sparing them from the fatigue of night work and banning undue exertion such as heavy weight lifting or exposure to the risk of poisoning from noxious substances, the legislator's aim has been, in fact, to safeguard the function of maternity and the welfare of future generations....

The regulations concerned directly with the protection of maternity have thus lost none of their significance and current applicability. It is with respect to maternity that women will always need special protection. It is necessary to protect not only

---

[1] Kogi et al. (1975).

[2] Pugh and McMahon (1962).

[3] Frazer (1947).

[4] Grandjean (1969).

[5] ILO (1975 c), p. 5.

the expectant mother but also her unborn child and the unweaned child from risks, such as risks of poisoning (lead, benzene, etc.), to which the mother's work might expose them.

CONCLUSIONS

As the conclusions to be set out here will be confined to the physiological, psychological and medical aspects of night work, they will call for subsequent supplementary conclusions in which account will be taken of other aspects of the question.

All those organs of the body which relate man to his environment (muscles, central nervous system, sensory organs, etc.) are subject to fatigue, that is to say that, after functioning for some time, they have to suspend their activity temporarily in order to replenish their stores of energy. That is why work, which is a typical instance of the relationship between man and the natural, technical and social environment, also gives rise to the phenomenon of fatigue and requires an alternation of exertion and rest.

The human body is, however, subject to circadian biological rhythms that have the general effect of activating it by day and de-activating it at night. In particular, the rhythms of some parts of the brain (reticular formation and hypothalamus) induce an alternation of a diurnal state of wakefulness conducive to activity and especially to work and of nocturnal sleep which corrects the fatigue of wakefulness.

In the case of the worker by day, there is a concurrence of the period of biological activation with the work schedule and of the period of de-activation of the brain with the hours of sleep. On the other hand, in the case of the night worker there is a discordance of periods in both cases: he has to work in a state of nocturnal de-activation involving extra exertion for an equal workload, and he has to sleep in a state of diurnal re-activation, making for sleep of an inferior quality and for insufficiently restorative sleep.

This twofold strain explains the over-fatigue and the fatigue disorders to which night workers are subject. The over-fatigue is revealed in a deterioration of some physiological, psychological and electroencephalographic indicators, a diminution of occupational output and an increase in the seriousness of accidents. When over-fatigue becomes chronic and when exhaustion of the hypothalamus becomes permanent, night work, whether regular or rotating, can give rise to a psychosomatic complaint taking the form either of a neurotic syndrome or of a digestive ulcer. In its rotating form, night work can cause, in addition, digestive disorders liable to development on their own or to combination with the preceding complaint.

Age and length of service are aggravating factors in night work: the psychological and physiological weakening caused by ageing increases the strain of night work, while the disturbances of sleep brought on by ageing further diminish the restorative powers of sleep by day. At the same time, the incidence of pathological disorders increases with length of service in night work so that there is no habituation to, but rather an increasing intolerance of, that kind of work, which ultimately has to be abandoned in most cases towards the age of 40 or 50.

On the other hand, sex plays no role, so that from the medical point of view there is no justification for protecting only women workers, except in so far as their function of reproduction is concerned because of the risks to the children.

Other individual factors bearing to a greater or lesser extent on tolerance of night work are thought to have been discerned, but there is not yet sufficient knowledge of this question for the adoption of methods of selection.

Thus the over-all conclusion which emerges from the present chapter is that night work is, in all its forms, abnormally fatiguing and liable to affect adversely the health of the worker. It would therefore be justifiable, as a general rule, to ban night work on medical grounds. Where there must be exceptions to that rule, as in the case of continuously operating industries, permanent public utility services, etc., the advisable course is to aim at a reduction of its duration. This suggestion is, however, still of hypothetical worth only: it calls for the confirmation of future experimental research, especially in the field.

EFFECTS OF NIGHT WORK ON FAMILY AND SOCIAL LIFE

2

The existence of stable biological rhythms that can be disturbed by night work was noted in Chapter 1, which also examined the effects of night work on health. The problem which those rhythms, when regarded as established facts, raise in practice for both workers and undertakings is, however, the wider one of the relations between work schedules and the various aspects of the life of the undertaking and of the private and social life of the workers.

The disturbances of family and social life caused by night work are at the root of one of the main criticisms of that work made by sociologists. The disturbances also affect the worker's occupational life and have repercussions too on the organisation of the civic environment, which is complicated by nocturnal work schedules.

In the studies of these aspects of night work that have been carried out, an attempt is made to determine the extent to which some workers endeavour to overcome or set aside the problem which night work raises in their family and social life and also to benefit from the advantages which night work may give them. Those studies also bring to light the repercussions of irregular work schedules and especially of night work on the workers' families and on the social organisation and the life of the community. The studies consist mainly of subjective investigations; they refer to experiences of particular situations that do not easily lend themselves to generalisations; they refer to individual perceptions of the advantages and inconveniences of night work; the workers' attitudes towards, and opinions about, their own situation do not necessarily correspond to previously ascertained physiological data but none the less constitute an integral part of the problem. An attempt will be made here to draw out of these studies their relevant features, to determine the extent to which they converge towards results that can be generalised or, on the contrary, diverge in their assessments, bearing in mind that night work pertains to a system that can assume many different forms. Night work can be practised regularly or in rotation and it is not always possible to isolate the respective effects of night work schedules and of rotation of the schedules, although night work always does play a role in these effects.

The present chapter will be concerned especially with the disruption of family life, psychological balance and the roles of the family, social life, use of leisure, working life and organisation of community life.

DISRUPTION OF FAMILY LIFE

The disturbances in family life are the inconveniences to which night workers and their families object most strongly. For example, the results of one inquiry show that 66 per cent of the workers on rotating work schedules considered that they were more inconvenienced in their family life than in any other respect, the percentage ranging from 56 in the case of workers on two eight-hour shifts (no night work) to 75 in the case of workers on three eight-hour shifts (work on rotating schedules with Sunday work). These figures clearly show the role played by night work in the inconvenience felt.[1]

Most of the investigators stress the negative effects of night work on family life. These affect the whole family: the worker, his wife and his children. It has been noted,[2] for example, that rotating night workers attach more importance than do others to family life, because it can contribute to their sense of poise: it is, for them, a source of appeasement and relaxation—except where, on the contrary, it is a cause of tension and conflict.

The effects of night work, whether regular or under rotating work schedules, seem to bear on two aspects of family life:[3]

— on the one hand, the practical organisation of day-to-day domestic life;
— on the other hand, the life of the family as a unit, including the relations between members of the family.

Day-to-day organisation of domestic life

The day-to-day organisation of domestic life is disrupted by the discordance between the timetable of the worker's schedule of work and his family's timetable. A night worker or a worker on rotating shifts will find [3] that he must:
— either conform to his family's routine, interrupting his sleep for the midday meal with them; or
— make his family conform to his own timetable, which is sometimes feasible if his family is small and especially if his wife has no outside work; or, again,
— follow a routine of his own, more or less independently of his family.

In any case, difficulties arise in the preparation and organisation of meals, in housework and in looking after the children. In the case of night work on

---

[1] Maurice and Monteil (1965).
[2] Chazalette (1973).
[3] Fourré (1962).

rotating schedules, these difficulties vary with the shift and accumulate during the cycle of shifts. Wives who were interviewed reported that they found the shift system a burden owing to the constant changes in mealtimes.[1]

In one investigation it was found that the rotating workers took part more frequently than other workers in household work and especially that they helped their wives more frequently.[2] The explanation may be that they had more time to spend at home with their wives, who did not go out to work. However, the finding points to a form of co-operation rather than to a division of household tasks between husband and wife.

The night worker's sleep by day can be disturbed by the activities of the members of his family [3] or his need for sleep can interfere with their freedom. These difficulties appear to grow with the number of children. An investigator found that difficulties had been experienced by 24 per cent of the families with one child, 40 per cent of those with two children and 50 per cent of those with five children, and that only one family in every 91 families did not seem to have altered its habits during the worker's rest, whereas all the other families held that his rest was troublesome to all the members of the family. Be that as it may, the atmosphere of the family is affected by the discomfort caused to the worker, who sleeps poorly, and to his family, who are not free to carry on their activities. The difficulties are not merely practical: they can cause family relations to suffer.[1]

Family relations

The disturbances of family life due to night work with rotating schedules, which is the most widely practised form of night work, are caused by:
— desynchronisation of activities with the rhythms of life;
— shift rotation, which involves constant changes.

These causes are not peculiar to the night shift, every shift having its own inconveniences; but they do have the effect of diminishing the number of hours spent together at home by all the members of the family and of making constant changes in the timing of those hours. It is especially at mealtimes that the members of a family form a unit; but, depending on its timing, shift work can reduce the number of meals which the worker can take with his family. It was found in an investigation carried out in France that 45 per cent of the workers on night shift could take the two main meals of the day with their families (though only at the cost of interrupting their sleep), but that one-quarter of the workers on afternoon shifts did not take any meals with their families.[4]

---

[1] Brown (1959).
[2] Guérin and Durrmeyer (1973).
[3] Brown (1959); Caillot (1959).
[4] Maurice and Monteil (1965).

For the same reasons, rotating night work raises difficulties—strongly resented by the majority of workers—in the exercise of parental responsibilities for the upbringing of the children. These difficulties arise especially during the period of afternoon or night work; workers on morning shifts can spend the evenings with their families, though not without interrupting their sleep if the morning shift begins early.

Rotating night work allows for various kinds of family life. Precise information on the effects of shift work on family life is, however, scarce. According to one inquiry, 33 per cent of the workers considered that shift work had its advantages; 43 per cent that it had its inconveniences; and 24 per cent that it had both advantages and inconveniences. The inconveniences most frequently mentioned were: insufficient time spent with the family (38 per cent), household noise (27 per cent), irregular rhythm of life (28 per cent). The advantages referred to the improvements in family life relating to the sharing of household work, activities in common and discussion. These advantages affected also the children: more time spent by the father with them; time for both parents to look after them or to take it in turns to do so.[1]

Thus it seems that the longer time which the night worker can spend at home is generally appreciated by both his wife and his children because it allows for more family life and for a better distribution of tasks within the family. The inconveniences, on the other hand, refer to the de-synchronisation of the rotating work schedules and the irregularity of the rhythms of life.

It is to be noted, however, that rotating work is appreciated by workers in particular cases: it enables those who are separated from their families to visit them by accumulating their days of rest, and it enables family units liable to breakdown to survive by reducing the number of hours spent together. Indeed, couples whose married life is already in difficulties may even aim at that system of work.

The only systematic investigations of family relations that have been made have been concerned with strains (measured by the divorce rate) in the married life of night workers. The results of these investigations are, however, contradictory. There have not been any objective studies showing the observed effects of night work on the education of the children. On the other hand, some studies have been undertaken for the purpose of ascertaining the psychological ill effects of changes in family relations caused by night work.

PSYCHOLOGICAL BALANCE AND ROLES PLAYED IN THE FAMILY

Studies of the psychological effects of night work have produced interesting results concerning the roles played in the family by, in particular, the husband or the father.[2] These results may be summarised as follows:

---

[1] Chazalette (1973).

[2] Mott et al. (1965).

In the first place, the harder it is for a worker to reconcile the demands of his working life with his responsibilities in private life, the more his psychological state suffers; his anxieties increase, he comes into growing conflict with himself and his self-respect declines. There is thus a relation between the worker's sense of his difficulties and his psychological equilibrium.

Second, when the interferences of occupational life with specific roles played in private life are considered more closely, it is found that the greater the disturbance of the worker's roles of husband, father and citizen, the more significantly those disturbances affect his psychological equilibrium.

Third, a question that arises is whether that observed basic connection between the disturbance of certain roles and mental health is at work whatever may be the individual worker's personal characteristics: his psychology, his family situation and his personal background. It has been found that that fundamental connection subsists whatever the individual worker's personal characteristics. Thus the fact that an individual worker may or may not show signs of neurosis leaves that basic connection unaffected.

On the other hand, the atmosphere of the individual worker's family does seem to exercise a definite, though not yet fully clarified, influence on his ability to withstand the psychological and social consequences of his work schedules. The effect of that factor is, however, obscure: it seems that an understanding attitude on the part of the worker's wife can conduce to his psychological resistance. On the other hand, it has not been confirmed that an uncompromising attitude on the part of the wife increases her husband's psychological strain. In any case, independent-mindedness on the part of the wife does conduce to the worker's psychological adaptation to night work.[1]

So far as the individual worker's personal background is concerned, it has been found that psychological disorders caused by the psychological and social consequences of the work schedules are all the more pronounced in relation to the youth or the level of education of a worker, or if he has young children to support, or if the degree of his seniority in his branch of activity is low, or if he is in poor health.

It follows from the foregoing that the psychological and social effects of night work affect the worker's psychological equilibrium to a degree depending on the psychological and social environmental conditions.

All the psychological and sociological investigations of the question have shown, furthermore, that the effect of night work on family life is strongly felt. This circumstance will have to be taken into account below when inquiry is made into modifications of work schedules and living conditions, as well as special measures to be considered in the event of discontinuation of the ban on night work for women. It has to be recognised, however, that the sense of satisfaction with family life is subject also to the influence of factors extraneous to occupational life and to family life, including, in particular, participation in social life.

---

[1] Chazalette (1973); see also Banks (1956).

DIFFICULTIES IN SOCIAL LIFE

Several studies [1] have noted the sense of malaise and isolation felt by the night worker. Some writers have even defined that sense as one of "social extinction". The sense is due largely to a discordance between the schedules of night workers and those of other workers, that is, to de-synchronisation of leisure times. That de-synchronisation is aggravated in the case of rotating work schedules owing to the constant changes of work times.

A distinction must be drawn here between informal and formal social relations.

Informal relations

There are several studies showing that night workers have the same informal social life as workers by day, although it is not so easy for them to see their friends. While there is no appreciable difference between rotating night workers and day workers in the number of their visits to friends, the former have fewer friends: their circle of friends is narrower owing to difficulties in making new friends.[2] Nevertheless, it was found in an inquiry [3] that 64 per cent of the night workers on rotating schedules who were interviewed had a limited social life (though the figure is not compared in the study to the percentage in a control group) and that 60 per cent of them felt that they were inconvenienced in their social life. It is to be noted that these informal relations are facilitated when there is no Sunday work. That day can then be devoted to the family and friends and provide the main opportunity for social relations.

The environment can also play a role in two opposite ways: the larger the number of workers on rotating schedules, the more difficult is it for them to meet friends but the less do they have the feeling of being on the fringe of social life. It seems, in a general way, that night work raises fewer problems when it is technically warranted and involves a large number of workers. It was found in an inquiry carried out in a small town in Britain that night work was tolerated or accepted because the majority of the inhabitants were involved in it.[4]

It seems, too, that the fact that, in a locality where there is a large number of night workers, some account is taken of their situation plays a decisive role in that regard.[3] Such workers become accustomed to their lot and find ways of organising their social life accordingly. On the other hand, where the practice of night work is not widespread or is comparatively recent, the night worker has to contend with greater difficulties because he feels deprived of local support.

---

[1] Maurice and Monteil (1965); Chazalette (1973).

[2] Mott et al. (1965).

[3] Chazalette (1973).

[4] Blakelock (1960).

In the case of rotating night work, short cycles of rotation, which appear to be practised more and more nowadays, disrupt social relations owing to difficulties in understanding the work calendar. A question that arises is whether a simple calendar of rotation that could be readily consulted might not greatly facilitate social relations. It has been suggested [1] that, at the beginning of each month, every worker should receive calendars indicating his periods of work—hence also his periods of leisure—which he could distribute to his family and friends. This practice is in fact in use today, though only in a small number of undertakings.

Formal relations

It is especially the workers' activities in groups (sports, trade unions, political, cultural, etc., pursuits) which suffer from night work. The night worker cannot take part regularly in such activities and sometimes is excluded from them, or excludes himself from them, if he cannot pursue them in a normal way.

Moreover, the more frequent the meetings of these groups, the more difficult participation in them becomes. In that respect the nature of the group activity plays a role. For example, membership of a local club or of a political party, with their comparatively rigid organisational structures, is more demanding than engaging in some sport or participating in the affairs of a local authority.

As a result, night workers rarely fill any management post; nor would it be easy for them to hold a post of responsibility in, for example, a trade union,[2] or in a cultural, sports or political group.

According to the results of an inquiry carried out in the United States,[1] the percentage of workers who are members of two voluntary associations is higher among day workers than among night workers. This difference is not affected by age and level of education. It was found also that wives of workers on rotating work schedules belonged to fewer associations than wives of workers on regular afternoon or night shifts, and that the posts held in these associations by workers with normal work schedules carried greater responsibility than those held by night workers. On the other hand, no difference between the two categories of worker was noted in the number of weekly hours devoted to membership of these associations.

Nevertheless, a study made in France [3] does not show any significant difference between workers with normal day schedules and night workers in their membership of associations. Social and cultural differences between France and the United States may account for this difference between the

---

[1] Mott et al. (1965).

[2] Bratt (1973).

[3] Maurice and Monteil (1965).

findings of the two inquiries, membership of a voluntary association being far more general in the United States than in France.

A final point to be noted is that no study has been made of the effects of night work on migrant workers. It is clear, however, that night work cannot but accentuate their isolation and impede their social integration.

USE OF LEISURE TIME

Nature of the occupation

Night work implies that the whole of each daily quota of work has to be performed uninterruptedly. This concentration of the time spent at work enables night workers to consolidate their free time so as to give them a morning or afternoon of leisure. This advantage is generally welcomed by the workers and constitutes an important factor of adaptation to night work. It is so regarded, according to one inquiry, by 61 per cent of the workers, while 38 per cent of them regard it as decisive.[1]

The leisure time activities are highly varied. Many night workers do odd jobs at home; others are interested mainly in gardening. A smaller proportion attach much importance to outdoor activities: sports, going for a walk and, in fewer cases, social and cultural pursuits.

The nature of the housing accommodation largely determines the type of leisure occupation, the individual house lending itself better than group housing to the utilisation of free time. Escapist behaviour has been found more frequently among night workers than among other workers. It is as if they had a greater need to shake off the strains of their life at work.[2] During their free time, night workers turn their thoughts more often than other workers to their work.[3] There are three reasons for that difference. A first reason is that, as the factory continues to work while they are resting, it is difficult for them to dismiss it completely from their minds. Second, as the end of a shift may occur while a task is being performed, the night worker may have the feeling of having left a job unfinished. Lastly, he may wonder during his hours of rest whether he forgot anything when hastily passing on the instructions to the following shift.

The night worker thus tends to fall back on types of leisure activity that he can pursue individually and irrespective of their normal times, such as odd jobs, gardening, fishing, reading, listening to the radio, and so on. Although these activities are much the same as those practised by workers whose interest is concentrated on their home rather than on the community,[4] inquiries have shown a clear sense of dissatisfaction, which is expressed in a feeling of being on the fringe of various activities. A distinction must be drawn, therefore,

---

[1] Chazalette (1973).
[2] Maurice and Monteil (1965).
[3] Guérin and Durrmeyer (1973).
[4] Maurice (1975).

between actual behaviour and the individual's awareness of that behaviour. It is the feeling of being unable to take part in some activity that is one of the important causes of the harmfulness of night work, even though that feeling is purely subjective.

Second jobs and women's work

The question of second jobs is a difficult one which has not often been studied. The prevailing view of those who have considered this question is that second jobs are found more frequently among night workers than among other workers. The fact that the schedule of night work leaves part of the daytime free may lead night workers to engage in a second activity either regularly or occasionally. Indeed, in many cases it is the prospect of a second job that may cause some workers to accept or choose night work. This is certainly the case in some countries with many workers who have kept their roots in the country and who find in the system of rotating work schedules a means of obtaining wage-earning employment while continuing to work their land. It is, moreover, these considerations which weigh in the balance when systems of rotation are set up after discussion with the workers.

For example, according to one investigation the proportion of workers having second jobs was found to be appreciably larger among workers with rotating schedules, whether with Sunday work (27 per cent of the subjects of the investigation) or without work on Sundays (33 per cent), than among workers employed on normal work by day (19 per cent) or among workers on regular shifts (12 per cent).[1] It is to be noted, however, that the sample of workers with rotating schedules was composed entirely of men, whereas nearly one-half of the workers in the two other samples were women, among whom a paid second job is certainly less common than among men. As for the nature of the second jobs, it varies with local labour market conditions.

According to another inquiry carried out in France only 9 per cent of the workers with rotating schedules had a second job of any consequence other than farming or stock-raising.[2]

It may be that the higher rate of second jobs among workers with rotating schedules than among other workers is due to the fact that they have few opportunities of working overtime.

It appears, furthermore, from yet another study that a worker on rotating schedules whose family needs a supplementary income tends to take on a second job rather than let his wife go to work.[3] His work schedule enables him to do so, whereas if his wife worked the whole of his family life would be upset and he himself might no longer retain the psychological equilibrium he needs in order to continue his rotating shift work. If his wife worked, his resistance to rotating work schedules would be undoubtedly severely impaired.

---

[1] Maurice and Monteil (1965).

[2] Chazalette (1973).

[3] Guérin and Durrmeyer (1973).

WORKING LIFE

Wages

There are no general regulations governing the remuneration of night work. For the same qualifications, the night worker's wages are higher than those of other workers because of the increased pay on Sundays and holidays (in the case of continuous operations) and of the food ration bonus paid daily during the night shift. For example, in the Swedish chemical industry the bonuses paid in respect of continuous operations represent from 18 to 20 per cent of the total wage bill.[1] According to a study made in France, the bonuses paid to workers on three-shift systems amount in many cases to one-quarter of the wage.[2] These are only illustrations: practice varies with the industry and with the country. The worker on rotating schedules has, however, additional expenses. A report published by the ILO[3] refers to the following sources of supplementary expenditure:

— need for supplementary meals;
— cost of fuel for the preparation of meals taken at home at times differing from those of the family meals;
— additional lighting and heating owing to early morning departures and late returns.

Yet it seems that the amount of additional expenses is smaller than the financial advantages from which night workers benefit.

The bonuses compensating for the hardship felt by the night worker can constitute, however, a deceptive lure in so far as they become indispensable to his family. He will then have to remain on night work even at the cost of over-fatigue because of the limited opportunities for transfer to other jobs without loss of remuneration. Transfers to normal daytime work in the same undertaking are not easily arranged. Nevertheless, some undertakings do allow for such transfers at the same wages upon completion of a certain number of years of night work. Trade unions have argued that night workers should be able to change their jobs upon medical advice without incurring any loss of wages.[4]

Worker relations

Workers on shift work generally feel that they belong occupationally to a special group within which relations with fellow workers are particularly close. It has been found that there is more cohesion within teams of workers during the night than by day.[5] Night workers also feel that, owing to the absence of certain supervisory staff, they enjoy more freedom than workers by day.

---

[1] Bratt (1973).
[2] Chazalette (1973).
[3] ILO (1952).
[4] See, for example, CFDT (1974).
[5] Maurice and Monteil (1965).

Many night workers also have a sense of special responsibility in ensuring the continuity of production. This feeling can create a barrier between day workers and night workers which causes some concern to trade unions.[1]

Moreover, a feeling of separation from the day-to-day life of the undertaking has been noted among night workers. They feel less well informed because the information that reaches them is mainly by word of mouth. They attach more importance than other workers to trade unionism and their complaints are more frequently made through their union representatives. Furthermore, most night workers consider that they do not benefit fully from the advantages offered by the undertaking, including, in particular, vocational training, especially in the case of courses given by outside bodies at times arranged for workers on normal daytime schedules. It is difficult for workers with rotating work schedules to attend such courses except, in the best of cases, at the cost of considerable personal exertion.

The passing on of instructions from one shift to the next can present difficulties that could have repercussions on safety. There are statistics to show that incidents and accidents occur most frequently at the beginning of a shift.

ORGANISATION OF COMMUNITY LIFE

Getting to and from work

Some workers live at a considerable distance from the large industrial centres. Some undertakings provide pick-up services. In other cases the workers have to use public transport, whose timetables, despite the adjustments which the large transport undertakings try to make, are not always suited to the work schedules. Even where, in the best of cases, there is a pick-up service, the coaches may make wide detours and are liable to be slow. It must not be overlooked that, under the most widely practised work schedules, getting-up times may be at 2 or 3 a.m. and the time of going to bed may be round about midnight. The time spent at work is thus considerably lengthened, and travel to and from work is all the more tiring when it takes place at night. It has been reported by some trade unions that the traffic accident rate is much higher among shift workers than among others, though they have not furnished any statistics. A question that arises is whether there should be some compensation for night travel on the grounds that it is more tiring than travel by day, in the same way as night work is better paid than work by day, or, alternatively, whether the time spent on night travel should be taken out of the work time.

A study carried out in France has shown that, whatever the amount of time spent on travel, night workers never consider that they live too far away from the place of work.[2] On the contrary, they want to live as far away as possible from their workplace so as to cut off their working life from their private and family life. Where the factory remains continuously at work, they cannot detach themselves from it completely if they live close to it.

---

[1] CFDT (1974).

[2] Guérin and Durrmeyer (1973).

Housing

The size of the home and its situation have an important effect on the quality of the worker's rest and on the family atmosphere. Sleep difficulties vary with the size of the home. According to an investigation made in France, these difficulties arise in 55 per cent of the cases where the family does not have two rooms (including the kitchen), 41 per cent of the cases where it has three rooms, 27 per cent of the cases where it has four rooms and only 7.6 per cent of the cases where it has five rooms.[1]

The living conditions of the home can either conduce to, or render more difficult, the adjustments needed to remedy the inconveniences of night work.[2]

Furthermore, the environmental situation of the shift worker's home plays an important role: a rural environment unquestionably helps his sleep.

The community

Whereas the rhythm of life is being increasingly organised collectively,[3] night work is introducing into that trend a factor of de-synchronisation. The weekly days of rest taken by rotation can then make for a more economic exploitation of community installations and infrastructures through the spreading out of the time during which they are used. The development of shift work in recent years has undoubtedly played an important part in the prolongation of the hours of community life (shopping and maintenance of transport and other services, etc., during night hours). As has already been noted, these developments of community life, while having obvious disadvantages, facilitate the adaptation of workers to night work.

OPINIONS ON NIGHT WORK

The close interdependence of the various aspects of night work that have been examined in this chapter and the inseparability of the individual's physiological and psychological functions must not be overlooked when considering opinions on night work. While general conclusions cannot be based solely on the social aspects of night work, these aspects nevertheless have to be taken into account.

Attitudes towards, and opinions on, night work are marked by two trends.[4]

There is, first, some uncertainty in workers' preferences. Not many workers hold any definite opinion, either favourable or unfavourable. In the majority of cases the worker puts up with night work, and writers on the subject note that a large proportion of night workers do not definitely object to night work

---

[1] Caillot (1959).

[2] Chazalette (1973).

[3] Grossin (1969).

[4] Maurice and Monteil (1965).

but tinge their acceptance of it with various considerations and hesitate to express a view. Opinions are not strongly held and can be changed by a reduction of working time or by grants of pecuniary advantages.

The same writers point out that, when the arguments for and against night work are expressed, a favourable attitude or a positive intention to continue on night work will be based on factors in the following order: free time, family life, wages, transport and social life. On the other hand, hesitation to continue on night work and especially a wish to abandon it will be based on factors in the following order: age, health, normal way of living, family life and social life. Every strategic plan of life [1] is closely related to the cultural patterns acquired in youth or from the groups to which the worker belongs or which he aspires to join: the greater the likelihood that night work will enable the worker to achieve his expectations or his plan, the more readily will it be accepted.

Second, workers display some attachment to the system which they know and practise, in which respect they show the usual resistance to change whether in work schedules or in the rate of rotation of shifts. [2] That resistance may be due also to the effect of the secondary factors which, as has been seen, play an important part in the psychological balance of the night worker. The numerous combinations of factors and the order of priority given to them will determine whether night work is found either endurable or intolerable [1] and will produce a variety of forms of adaptation and a diversity of reactions.

It is to be noted, however, that most of the studies that have been made find that the majority of workers are, on the whole, dissatisfied with night work and are critical of that system of work.

CONCLUSIONS

An attempt has been made in this chapter to assess the main psychological and social effects of night work, both regular and under rotating schedules. The psychological and sociological effects of the organisation of night work have significant repercussions on the worker's mental poise. Although the evidence consists more of alleged complaints than of objective findings, it is clear enough that there is also some disruption of the family unit due to unusual work schedules and especially to their irregularity (rotating work schedules and rotating periods of rest in the case of continuous operations). Investigations have also shown that adjustments are possible, since adaptation is, ultimately, closely connected with personal factors which in many cases are extraneous to the work. Nevertheless, that adaptation is, in many cases, achieved only at the cost of compromises that are difficult to make lasting.

---

[1] Chazalette (1973).

[2] Maurice and Monteil (1965).

These conclusions must be extended to a wider social context. It is the disturbances of family relations which are the most keenly felt and which are, in many cases, tolerated only because the night worker's wife does not have a paid job outside the home. The night worker's family background exercises a decisive influence on his psychological equilibrium.

The situation would be fundamentally altered if the night worker's wife had to work under the same system as her husband, since she has to bear heavy family responsibilities. It has been shown in this connection that any extension of night work, whether regular or under rotating work schedules, to women would call in question stereotyped notions of the roles of the sexes in society and of models of family life and would call for a redefinition of the role of the family relative to that of other institutions, especially the school.

These observations should lead to a search for new forms of organisation of night work involving a reduction of working time so as to achieve a better reconciliation of work with social and family responsibilities.

The desirable rearrangements could not be made, however, at the individual level alone. The solution should bring about reforms extending beyond the range of the undertaking, and this would necessitate the adoption of a concerted social policy in this area.

Thus the organisation of night work must be regarded as one of the forms of over-all distribution of working time,[1] which must be thought out again as a whole and lead to a redefinition of long-established patterns.

---

[1] de Chalendar (1973).

ERGONOMIC ASPECTS OF PROBLEMS OF NIGHT WORK ORGANISATION AND STAFFING

3

As has been seen, night work is harmful to the well-being and health of the worker. The extent of the damage may vary, however, with certain factors relating to the organisation and nature of the work and the characteristics of the worker. The ergonomics of night work, while not constituting an essential feature of the present study, will be briefly considered in this chapter—first of all, and especially, from the medical point of view, then in relation to the sociological aspects of the problem, and lastly in a review of the principal proposals for an improvement of the conditions of night work and of shift work.

MEDICO-ERGONOMIC ASPECTS

If a night worker becomes tired and then ill, it will be because the circadian rhythm of his biological activation conflicts with the rhythm of his work. Consequently, there would be no medical problem if that worker could invert his biological rhythm so as to make it coincide with his work rhythm.

It has been seen, however, that for several reasons complete inversion cannot be achieved in the case of industrial night work. A first reason is that the occupational factors of synchronisation can entrain only some of the biological rhythms but not the others. Next, that entrainment is not complete, the maxima remaining diurnal. Lastly, that relative adjustment vanishes as soon as there is a return to a normal schedule of work or of rest, that is, after a week at the latest.

In default of a complete inversion that cannot be achieved, a question that arises is whether a useful function is performed by that partial adjustment, which dissociates the biological rhythms entrained by the occupational factors of nocturnal synchronisation from the biological rhythms which remain subject to the diurnal factors of synchronisation attributable to the family and the community. It does seem that such dissociation is, itself, pathogenic: it is those night workers who suffer most frequently from disorders who respond best to the entrainment of occupational work schedules by further reducing the amplitude of their nyctohemeral thermic variations.[1]

Rotating versus regular shifts

The foregoing suggests that, from the medical point of view, the two forms of night work—regular and by rotation—are approximately the same, except in the case, to be considered below, of very rapid rotation. For example, it has been shown in the case of the subjects of an experiment who did one week of day work and then three weeks of night work that "during the first days after the phase shifting of the working and sleeping times, the minima of the functions had a phase which differed greatly from the expected phase" and that "these differences in phase decreased up to the end of the three weeks of night shift in most functions"; "large differences in the phase of different functions which persisted till the end of the experiment" were, however, observed.[2] Yet some writers attach more importance, from the medical point of view, to regular night work than to rotating night work.[3] In the same way, when workers on rotating night shifts are compared with regular night workers, it is found that the former show a decline in reaction time and an increased excretion of catecholamines which are not shown by the latter.[4] The same alterations of reaction time have been found, however, among regular night workers,[5] while others have found that the nocturnal output of rotating shifts is higher than that of regular shifts.[6] Thus the question is still controversial.

Periodicity of shift rotation

Opinions differ on the desirable periodicity of shift rotation. Those who think that it is possible or even desirable to bring about an inversion in the biological rhythms want it to be slow, while those who do not think that inversion is possible or wish to avoid it want the periodicity to be rapid. Schools of thought vary from those who recommend shift rotation every two months to those who advocate rotation every day. It has also been recommended that the timing of the shifts should be advanced every day by 30 minutes with a view to avoiding all biological discordances. It is, however, easy to imagine the family and social problems which such a measure would raise. The most common practice in industry, whether in the case of semi-continuous operations allowing for Sunday rest or in the case of continuous operations, is weekly shift rotation, though there is a tendency in the United States, for example,

---

[1] Andlauer and Fourré (1965).

[2] Rutenfranz et al. (1975).

[3] Uhlich (1957).

[4] Pátkai et al. (1975).

[5] Solovieva and Gambashidze (1960).

[6] Murrell (1965).

to make use also of slower fortnightly or monthly shift rotations.[1] Recent studies recommend faster shift rotation every two or three days. When workers on fast shift rotation are compared with workers on weekly shift rotation, it is found that there are fewer cases of ill effects on health among the former.[2] Although that difference has not always been observed,[3] poor adaptation and difficulties of adjustment of the rhythms have nevertheless been observed even in the case of shift rotation every two days.[4] Others consider that the biological rhythms (body temperature) begin to invert only from the third night of work, which would make it desirable to stop night work after 48 hours.

In a word, the prevailing tendency today is to recommend fast shift rotation, although the merit of that recommendation has not yet been finally demonstrated.

Work schedules

From the medical and family points of view, what counts is the crucial clock time between the night and morning shifts. If it is early—at, for example, 4 [5] or 5 a.m. (allowing for the time needed to go to and from work) the night shift worker will have adequate morning sleep and may even be able to take the midday meal with his family without unduly curtailing his sleep; but the morning shift worker will suffer a premature awakening which, especially if he is a worry-prone introvert, may deeply disturb his night sleep. When the worker's own assessment of that situation is analysed,[6] the two forms of fatigue are contrasted: night shift fatigue and morning shift fatigue. The former is due mainly to over-exertion in the performance of work during a period of biological de-activation, while the latter, which occurs among workers on a system of two eight-hour shifts who have to get up early and which is usually more visible than the former, is due mainly to the cutting off of the last part of sleep when paradoxical sleep is most intense.[7]

If the shifts change at a later hour—6 or 7 a.m. or later, as is the practice in some continuously operating services—the morning shift worker will be in good form but the night shift worker will suffer double stress from working in a period of de-activation and from having sleep delayed until noon owing to the conflict between the need for sleep and the need to satisfy his appetite for food, the latter need reflecting, no doubt, not so much the body's requirement as a social and ecological synchronisation.

Nevertheless, examination of the relations between the beginning of the shift and coal mine accidents has shown an appreciable fall in the accident rate when the beginning of the shift is changed from 6 to 7 a.m.[8]

---

[1] Maurice (1975).

[2] Murrell (1965); Andlauer and Fourré (1965).

[3] Barhad and Pafnote (1970).

[4] Gavrilescu et al. (1966).

[5] Andlauer (1969).

[6] Reinberg, quoted in Bugard (1974), Vol. 1, pp. 50-51.

[7] Dement (1960); Jouvet (1962).

[8] Wild and Theis (1967).

Conclusions

The harmfulness of night work cannot be appreciably diminished by organisational changes which do not reduce its duration. Moreover, opinions differ on the purpose to be achieved. There are those who look for an adjustment of the biological rhythms to the night work schedules. (The adjustment never amounts to complete inversion. It is confined to a narrowing of the amplitude of the circadian variation of some, but not all, indicators and it vanishes on the first day of rest under a normal work schedule.) Others consider that that adjustment, by de-synchronising the biological rhythms from each other, has a traumatic effect on the body. The former advocate regular shifts or slowly rotating shifts, while the latter recommend fast rotation. Another problem that cannot be satisfactorily solved is that of the choice of the crucial timing of the change from the night to the morning shift. If the hour is very early, it is the morning worker who suffers, while, if it is later, it is the night worker who suffers.

SOCIO-ERGONOMIC ASPECTS

Rotating versus regular shifts

A distinction was drawn above between two of the many different systems of organisation of shifts that are practised: regular night shifts and rotating shifts. In some countries, such as France, only a small proportion of the night workers are not on rotating shifts; in other countries, such as the United States, the practice of regular shifts is more widespread.

In the case of rotating shifts, each shift has its advantages and inconveniences from the social point of view:

— The morning shift (for example, from 6 a.m. to 2 p.m. or from 5 a.m. to 1 p.m.) enables the worker to take his evening meal with his family and to take part in family and social life. Although favoured by many workers, this shift is sometimes stated to be very tiring, especially if it starts very early in the morning (e.g. at 4 a.m.). Nevertheless, it allows for more free time. The work schedules in use in the United States (8 a.m. to 4 p.m.) cannot be compared with the very different work schedules in use in Europe. In the United States the 8 a.m. to 4 p.m. shift is the one that is least disadvantageous to the worker. It enables him to participate normally in family and social life and to carry on with his outside activities in the evening.[1]

— The afternoon shift, which is usually from 1 p.m. to 9 p.m. or from 2 p.m. to 10 p.m., appears to be the most disadvantageous from the social point of view, for it restricts family life, the worker being at home when his children are not there and vice versa. Nor can the worker take part in any evening activity. The afternoon shift is nevertheless favoured by many

---

[1] Mott et al. (1965).

workers because it leaves plenty of time for sleep. Indeed, many workers on rotating shifts regard the afternoon shift as a means of recuperation.

— The night shift is obviously the one that raises most problems because of its repercussions on the family atmosphere. When it begins at 9 or 10 p.m. it precludes all social activity in the evening. (In the United States the night shift, which begins at midnight, cuts off less of the evening.) On the other hand, the night shift leaves a good deal of free time during the day. The atmosphere of night work and the increased pay make the night shift acceptable and it is sometimes preferred to other shifts for these reasons.

The system of rotating shifts involves a succession of all these advantages and inconveniences and, in addition, the difficulties which the periodical changes cause in household arrangements.

Several inquiries have shown a preference on the part of workers for regular night work.[1] They prefer it on grounds of less fatigue, regularity of daily life and health. Regular shifts can enable the worker to move from one shift to another, which is not feasible under the system of rotation. In the United States the worker can change his shift according to his length of service in the undertaking. The choice is not then confined only to a change to a normal daytime shift, which usually involves a loss of pay, and night work can be reserved, so far as possible, for volunteers.

Nevertheless, the most widely practised system is that of rotating work shifts, which is a compromise between advantages and inconveniences. Some writers consider that the system of rotating work shifts may be less costly to the undertaking than regular shift work.[2]

Periodicity of shift rotation

A question that arises in connection with the system of rotating work shifts is that of the desirable rate of changes of shifts. It is mainly the physiologists who discuss the choice between slow and rapid rotation. Sociologists cannot easily take part in that discussion on the basis of existing studies, which show that the workers' preference goes to the system to which they are accustomed. It may be noted, however, that slow rotation, which involves less frequent changes, allows for a more regular family life but for days of rest at longer intervals.

It seems that the system that can be regarded as extremely desirable is one of simple and regular rotation so as to allow for some regularity in family and social life and for ease of planning of activities and social relations. However, it is to be noted that, where the hours of shift have been reduced and a fifth shift has been introduced, the system practised allows for compensating periods of rest whose periodicity and duration can take many different forms.

---

[1] Mott et al. (1965); Maurice and Monteil (1965); Chazalette (1973).
[2] Mott et al. (1965).

Work schedules

The work schedules should be arranged so as to allow for some social and family life. Moreover, as has already been noted, inability to take part in family meals is greatly resented.

Under systems of three eight-hour shifts, the starting times of the shifts vary in Europe between 4 a.m., noon and 8 p.m., and 6 a.m., 2 p.m. and 10 p.m.

The earliest schedules can be a hardship to workers on morning shifts who spend the evening with their families (which is not feasible with any other shift), though they do enable him to take his meals in the middle of the day and in the evening with his family. The latest shifts, while satisfactory as regards the rest of a worker on the morning shift, involve changes in mealtimes.

In the United States the most widely practised shifts begin at, respectively, 8 a.m., 4 p.m. and midnight. The afternoon shift raises serious problems in that it does not leave the worker with any time to see his family.

Shift work schedules that would facilitate social and family life could be obtained by reducing the daily hours of work—a possibility that has hitherto received little attention. A six-hour shift has been proposed,[1] but most workers prefer a shorter working week to a day's work of less than eight hours.[2] In a saltpetre works at Koping in Sweden daily work was at first organised in four six-hour shifts. At the request of the women workers, it was reorganised in three eight-hour shifts. It is to be noted, however, that only 28 hours a week were worked.[3] There can be no doubt that the increasing length of journeys to and from work does not operate in favour of decreases in daily hours of work. Nevertheless, six-hour periods of work beginning at, say, 6 a.m., noon, 6 p.m. and midnight respectively would enable the worker to take his main meals at home.

The adoption of bold measures of reduction of hours of shift work, such as the 28-hour week referred to above, with maintenance of the wage level, would allow for more satisfactory arrangements, two examples of which may be given.

In the first case, there would be a series of fast rotations of shifts: the worker would have two eight-hour days of work and two days of rest on regular shifts in the morning or in the afternoon or at night according to his choice. This would be a 28-day cycle comprising 14 days of work, with a weekly average of 28 hours of work. This rotation of work and rest would allow adequate time for recuperation after each round of work, even at night, and for normal family life during at least half the time. Each cycle would include two free Sundays and one free weekend.

In the other case, the week would be divided into two periods of three-and-a-half days each. With eight daily hours of work, this arrangement could

---

[1] Carpentier (1969).

[2] Maurice (1975).

[3] Bratt (1973).

provide for three-and-a-half free days a week. Married couples where both spouses are at work could work either during the same periods or at different times so as to ensure a better distribution of responsibilities in the household and for the education of the children.

Although these are merely illustrations of what could be done, they show that original and positive solutions could be found if substantial reductions of the weekly hours of work were adopted.

SOME DESIRABLE REARRANGEMENTS

Since no system of night work, however organised, can be regarded as satisfactory from the physiological point of view, there is not much scope for any ergonomic arrangement of night work. There are two kinds of action that can be taken.[1]

In the first place, there can be a reduction of the number of workers who have to work at night. To that end, technical research must be directed towards the perfecting of automated processes that can be readily interrupted or slackened and the definition and distribution of operations and tasks must be so organised as to relieve the night shifts, the object being to limit very strictly the need for workers between 10 p.m. and 5 a.m.

Second, there can be a diminution of the harmful effects and discomforts of night work for such night workers who must remain, so as to reduce the number and difficulty of early transfers, allow a normal development of the working life of night workers and facilitate their family and social life.

Apart from the organisation of work shifts, there are various factors that can be modified with a view to diminishing the ill effects of night work. The main adjustments that have been proposed in studies of this question are described below. Due regard must be had to individual and social reactions when these proposed adjustments, whichever they may be, are introduced.

Reduction of weekly hours of work and of duration of assignment to night work; lowering of age of retirement

The wishes most frequently expressed by night workers with regard to the organisation of working time reveal two principal concerns: the reduction of hours of work, and the lowering of the age of retirement.

The reduction of hours of work would seem to be a logically more satisfactory compensation than financial compensation, because only an improvement in opportunities for rest can remedy the fatigue of night work. As for the age of retirement, long service aggravates difficulties as a result of the accumulation of residual fatigue and of diminished resistance and makes it desirable to prescribe an upper age limit. In France, for example, the trade unions have formulated various claims on behalf of night workers, including the following:

---

[1] Carpentier and Wisner (1976); Durafour (1976).

the reduction of hours of work to 40 a week, with the introduction of a fifth shift; the progressive reduction of hours of work to 36 and then to 33 a week; the lowering of the retirement age proportionately to the number of years spent on night work without a reduction of the amount of the pension. They have also demanded an increase in the number of workers per shift so as to allow for a more elastic system, a larger number of free weekends and more freedom of choice of compensatory periods of rest. While such measures would provide a partial solution of certain problems, they would lead also to an increase in the numbers of workers and families having to bear the consequences of night work. A last point to be noted is that a system of reduced weekly hours of night work, irrespective of the number of shifts, is already in force in some countries (Norway, Spain and Sweden).[1] Similar claims have been made in the United Kingdom, the United States and other countries. Finally, as has already been mentioned, various proposals and experiments have been based on reduced schedules (six-hour shifts, 28-hour week, and so on).

Diminution of the continuity of rotating work shifts; increased occupational mobility

Rotations of periods of shift work and of normal daytime work schedules have been proposed. The daytime work schedules could be devoted partly to special tasks such as maintenance and safety. In that way, the worker would work sometimes normally by day and sometimes in rotating shifts and would be employed on at least two different jobs. That system, which has already been adopted in some undertakings, offers several advantages from the worker's occupational point of view: fuller and multi-purpose training, opportunity of transfer after a certain age (50, for example) or a certain period of service in work shifts; but it also raises some problems of psychological and physiological adaptation, especially when the worker returns to shift work.[2]

Introduction of elasticity in work schedules

There could be a general policy of elastic work schedules, for which examples already exist in experiments with flexible hours. This flexibility should be extended also to school hours, so as to make possible family contacts on days of rest and at mealtimes, and also to social activities (entertainments, use of sports equipment, leisure, etc.). The policy would bring about de-synchronised distributions of work time and other time within a framework that might be no longer daily but weekly or yearly.

Improvement of transport, housing and meals at the workplace

There is common agreement among all those who have studied the question of night work that there is room for improvement in means of transport

---

[1] Klein (1970).
[2] Carpentier (1969).

(greater comfort, faster services) and in housing (sound-proofing, sufficiency of accommodation), as well as in the provision of facilities for nourishment at the workplace.

All the measures that have been considered in this chapter, while relating to the organisation of night work, concern also the broader question of the organisation of community life and the distribution of time spent at work and other time. All of them imply a social concept of night work that would have to be examined.

CONCLUSIONS

Every industrial society generates—and must then settle—a conflict between its functions of production and of the protection of the producer, between the needs of the economy and the biological and psychological requirements of the workers, and between the demands of industrial growth and the quality of individual and social life.

That conflict concerns both the time spent on production and the method of production; but the duration of the work was regulated before the work itself was regulated. The difficulties of flow-production have been due as much to the rhythms imposed on it as to the fragmentation of operations. Moreover, while recent technological trends towards automation have, in many cases, improved the quality of a process, they have also tended to increase the temporal difficulties. If, it is argued, equipment that rapidly becomes obsolete is to pay for itself, it must be used uninterruptedly, so that there has to be night work, whether regular or in rotating shifts. Hence, in the use of time, it is increasingly the machine that is mathematically setting the pace: machine time is prevailing over the passage of time for human beings.

Thus, to the problems of classic ergonomics, mechanisation and automation are adding "chrono-ergonomic" problems which might be defined as the problems of adapting the rhythms and cycles of production to the biological, psychological and social rhythms and cycles of human beings.

Chrono-ergonomics, like any other ergonomics, is bound to be comprehensive and multi-disciplinary—all the more so because the effect of taking into account the temporal dimension of the human and social problems of labour is to dismantle the barriers that artificially separated life at work from the rest of living, the factory from the community, and ergonomics, in its strict sense, from ecology.

It is from that broad angle of an "ecology of man at work" [1] that the present study has been prepared.

---

[1] Expression proposed by S. Pacaud in Scherrer et al. (1967).

The diversity of aspects of the question has led to a division of this study on night work into several parts. An introduction concerned especially with its technical and economic aspects is followed, first of all, by an objective approach to its psychological, physiological and medical aspects and then, in the manner of the social sciences, by an examination of the individual worker's experience of that method of work and of the attitudes of social groups towards that method. These divisions of the subject-matter, convenient though they are for purposes of exposition, cannot be retained in a concluding synthesis. It is now the whole question of man at grips with the stresses of night work that must be looked at comprehensively.

This consolidating approach to the facts can be organised around a few general propositions.

1. Night work, as at present practised, always causes fatigue and also, in many cases, a psychosomatic occupational disorder (neuroses and digestive ulcers) to which the practice of rotation can add specific digestive disorders. Moreover, the mental load involved in a task and the ageing of the worker can constitute aggravating factors. Again, night work disturbs family and social life. A growing number of workers object to it. Although the experts stress that technical and economic necessities require recourse to shift work, employers nevertheless side with trade union organisations of employees in advocating limited use of it [1] and measures designed to prevent its harmful effects.[2] In a word, night work is medically harmful and raises some contrasting social issues: while meeting certain social needs, it also raises some difficulties in the social life of the workers subjected to it.

2. In the case of women night workers, it is to be expected that the disturbances mentioned above will be aggravated, not by lesser biological and psychological aptitude for night work, but by the social usages which require from them both industrial and household work.

3. The explanation of the disorders caused by night work lies in the fact that man's circadian biological rhythms (that is, the rhythms with a period of about 24 hours) are no longer synchronised, as in the case of other mammals, with the alternation of daylight and nocturnal darkness, but with work schedules, on the one hand, and the timetables of family and social life, on the other. In the case of a day worker, there is a concurrence of phase between these two variables so that the biological rhythms are simultaneously and synergically entrained by both of them: diurnal activation fits the body to occupational, social and family activities, while nocturnal de-activation restores it from the fatigues of wakefulness. In the case of the night worker, there is a discordance of phase between the work schedules, which become nocturnal, and the social and family timetables, which remain diurnal. Cleavages then

---

[1] Conseil national du patronat français (French National Employers' Organisation): Model agreement of 17 March 1975.

[2] OECD, Joint Meeting of Experts on Team Work, Paris, 11-13 December 1973.

appear among the biological rhythms: some of them, such as the heartbeat, tend to give way to the entrainment of the work schedules, while others, such as the body temperature and the secretion of digestive juices, continue to be synchronised with the timetables of the family and the community. As a result, there is never any real inversion of the biological rhythms but merely a narrowing in the range of some of them—but not of others, so that they are no longer in harmony. There are good grounds today for assuming that this disruption of the temporal unity of the body is in itself pathogenic.

4. In the light of the foregoing, it is easier to understand both the divergencies in the attempts made by writers on the subject to devise methods of organising night work and the consistent failures of those attempts.

There are those who advocate either regular night work or slow rotation of night shifts, their aim being to de-synchronise the biological rhythms from the social and family timetables in order to re-synchronise them with nocturnal work schedules. They succeed only partially and then only by disrupting, as has just been shown, the temporal harmony of the body. These writers then feel tempted to prevent the disruption by adapting the social and family timetables to the work schedules, that is, by nocturnalising the activities of the family and of the community. Even if that were feasible, at any rate hypothetically, nothing would be solved because it would be the diurnal work that would be out of phase with biological rhythms that had become inverted and predominantly nocturnal. Yet it is to be noted incidentally that that is nevertheless the direction, or rather the dead end, towards which are headed proposals for dormitory towns with night-time activities, night-time nurseries, etc., leading ultimately to pollution of the whole community by the ill effects of industrially motivated night work.

The authors of some other studies advocate short rotations of night work, forgoing entrainment of the biological rhythms, which remain synchronised with the diurnal social and family timetables but become *ipso facto* out of phase with the nocturnal work schedules, thereby raising once again the initial problem of work during a period of de-activation and sleep during a period of re-activation.

The real difficulty thus clearly appears: the overriding requirement is that human activity, like that of all the higher animals, shall conform to a daily cycle of 24 hours during which 12 hours of activity are followed by 12 hours of rest and sleep. This alternation ought to apply simultaneously and synchronously both to factory life and to the life of the community. As they are in breach of that law, continuous or semi-continuous work schedules cannot be regarded as either biologically or sociologically acceptable.

5. Since no organisational arrangement seems capable at present of eliminating the harmfulness of night work, the only measures that can be taken for the prevention of the medical disorders and social and family disturbances caused by that kind of work must consist in a very strict limitation of night work for all workers, both women and men, and in a substantial

reduction of the duration of such work in cases where there are sufficiently good grounds for practising it.

It has been shown that the practice of night work distorts the system of wages and the conditions of economic competition. If the inequality which night work creates between workers, undertakings and countries is to be eliminated, night work must be either practised in all countries and for all types of activity or, by means of international measures and instruments, reduced to the minimum generally held to be indispensable. What is known of the harmfulness and disadvantages of night work suggests that the latter solution is the only one that can be recommended for the purpose of protecting the health and safeguarding the family life of the workers.

It has been shown also that the present regulations governing night work result in discriminations between men and women in their choices of employment and in the development of their working life.

The need for special protection of women with respect to certain general conditions of work is always warranted by reason of the woman's role as a mother. Yet the harmful effects and inconveniences of night work are felt equally by women and by men. A system of protection applicable only to women is insufficient as well as occupationally discriminatory. Regulations governing night work should be the same, therefore, for women and men.

Night work should be banned wherever its practice is motivated solely by the financial consideration of making costly equipment pay for itself more quickly. In other cases (including, in particular, cases of continuously operating industries and of permanent public utility services) studies should be made of the effects of a limitation of the duration of night work which would both alleviate the fatigue of night work and provide during the same or the following night for restorative sleep. It would be particularly desirable to carry out studies of technical processes and measures whereby machinery could be brought to a halt and then rapidly started up again or whereby physical and chemical processes could be slowed down or accelerated, thus providing for appreciable interruptions or decelerations of night work.

6. Apart from the measures proposed above, it will be useful to carry out multi-disciplinary and, if possible, internationally co-ordinated investigations designed to bridge the existing gaps in knowledge in the field of chrono-ergonomics. Such investigations would be concerned especially with the following questions: the unequal entrainment of biological rhythms by the occupational and social factors of synchronisation, the resulting de-synchronisation of the rhythms with each other and its psychological, physiological and medical effects; the long-term effects of night work on both sexes; the individual factors of ability and inability to endure night work; the effects of psychotropic drugs and stimulants on night workers' behaviour; the dividing up of work schedules and the periodicity of rotations; and the particular problems raised by some types of employment and by the conditions, especially climatic, prevailing in various geographical regions.

7. The recent extension of the practice of night work is due mainly to a desire to amortise as quickly as possible equipment that is highly mechanised or automated, costly and threatened with obsolescence. While this concern is no doubt worth planning for by the undertaking, the economic calculation which it may make seems narrowly based when account is taken of those indirect costs of night work which are borne, not only by the night workers themselves (threats to health, well-being and family and social responsibilities), but also by their families and by the community as a whole (public health expenditure, social security benefits, temporal disorganisation of community life and of the tertiary sector). As a result, both above and below the level of the undertaking night work is being called in question again by the workers, on the one hand, and, on the other hand, by some employers and in some governmental quarters. It is to be expected that this questioning will weigh more and more heavily in government policies and in international recommendations as the post-industrial society develops and as new systems of values come into operation.

BIBLIOGRAPHY

Abbreviations :

Arch. mal. prof. = *Archives des maladies professionnelles, de médecine du travail et de sécurité sociale* (Paris, Masson).

Int. J. Chronobio. = *International Journal of Chronobiology* (London, New York and Paris, Gordon and Breach Science Publishers), Vol. 3, 1975, No. 1.

PUF = Presses Universitaires de France (Paris).

Aanonsen, A. 1959. "Medical problems of shift-work", in *Industrial Medicine and Surgery* (Chicago, Industrial Medicine Publishing Co.), Sep. 1959, pp. 422-427.

Agnew, H. W., Jr.; Webb, W. B.; Williams, R. L. 1966. "The first night effect: An EEG study of sleep", in *Psychophysiology* (Baltimore, Md., Williams and Wilkins), Jan. 1966, pp. 263-266.

Andersen, E. J. 1958. "The main results of the Danish medico-psycho-social investigation of shiftworkers", in *Proceedings of the XII International Congress on Occupational Health, Helsinki, 1-6 July 1957* (Helsinki), pp. 135-136.

Andlauer, P. 1969. "Différentes modalités du travail en équipes alternantes", in *Réunion de chronobiologie appliquée à l'hygiène de l'environnement : Compte rendu* (Paris, Fondation A. de Rothschild).

— ; Fourré, L. 1962. *Aspects ergonomiques du travail en équipes alternantes* (Strasbourg, Centre d'études de physiologie appliquée au travail).

— ; — . 1965. "Le travail en équipes alternantes", in *Revue française du travail* (Paris, Ministère du Travail), Oct.-Dec. 1965, pp. 35-50.

— ; Metz, B. 1967. "Travail en équipes alternantes", in J. Scherrer (ed.): *Physiologie du travail : ergonomie* (Paris, Masson), Vol. II, pp. 272-281.

Aschoff, J. 1963. "Comparative physiology: Diurnal rhythms", in *Annual Review of Physiology* (Palo Alto, Calif., Annual Reviews Inc.), Vol. 25, pp. 581-600.

— . 1970. "Circadiane Periodik als Grundlage des Schlaf-Wach Rhythmus", in W. Baust (ed.): *Ermüdung, Schlaf und Traum* (Stuttgart, Wissenschaftlicher Verlag), pp. 59-98.

Baekeland, F.; Lasky, R. 1966. "Exercise and sleep patterns in college athletes", in *Perceptual and Motor Skills* (Missoula, Mont., Southern Universities Press), Vol. 23, pp. 1203-1207.

— ; Hartmann, E. 1970. "Sleep requirements and the characteristics of some sleepers", in E. Hartmann (ed.): *Sleep and dreaming* (Boston, Mass., Little, Brown), pp. 33-43.

Banks, O. 1956. "Continuous shift work: The attitudes of wives", in *Occupational Psychology* (London, National Institute of Industrial Psychology), Apr. 1956, pp. 69-84.

Barhad, B.; Pafnote, M. 1970. "Contributions à l'étude du travail en équipes alternantes", in *Le travail humain* (Paris, PUF), Vol. 33, Nos. 1-2, pp. 1-20.

Bartoli, H. 1957. *Sciences économiques et travail* (Paris, Dalloz).

Begoin, J. 1958. "Le travail et la fatigue; la névrose des téléphonistes et des mécanographes", in the quarterly *La raison* (Paris), Nos. 20-21, 1st quarter 1958.

Benoît, O. 1976. "Rythme veille-sommeil et modes d'existence", in *Revue du praticien* (Paris), 11 May 1976, pp. 1945-1954.

Berger, R. J.; Olley, P.; Oswald, I. 1962. "The EEG, eye-movements and dreams of the blind", in *Quarterly Journal of Experimental Physiology* (Cambridge, Heffer), Vol. 14, pp. 183-186.

Bjerner, B.; Holm, A.; Swensson, A. 1955. "Diurnal variation in mental performance: A study of three-shift workers", in *British Journal of Industrial Medicine* (London, British Medical Association), Apr. 1955, pp. 103-110.

Blakelock, E. 1960. "A new look at the new leisure", in *Administrative Science Quarterly* (Ithaca, NY, Cornell University), No. 4, pp. 446-467.

Bloch, V. 1966. "Les niveaux de vigilance et l'attention", in *Traité de psychologie expérimentale* (Paris, PUF), Vol. III, Ch. IX, pp. 79-122.

Bonjer, F. H. 1961. "Physiological aspects of shiftwork", in *Thirteenth International Congress on Occupational Health, New York, 25-29 July 1960: Proceedings* (New York), pp. 848-849.

Bratt, L. 1973. "Shift work: Length of working day", in OECD: *New patterns for working time: International conference, Paris, 26th-29th September 1972: Supplement to the final report* (Paris).

Brown, H. G. 1959. *Some effects of shiftwork on social and domestic life* (Hull University, Department of Economics and Commerce).

Browne, R. C. 1955. *The day and night performance in industry.* Report to the Fifth Conference of the Society of Biological Rhythms (Stockholm), No. 61.

Brusgaard, A. 1949. *Medizinske vurderinger av såkalt helseskadelig arbeid, saerlig skiftarbeid* (Oslo).

Buffet, A. 1963. "Statistiques et service de quart dans une raffinerie de pétrole", in *Arch. mal. prof.*, Vol. 24, Nos. 1, 2, 3, pp. 218-221.

Bugard, P. 1960. *La fatigue* (Paris, Masson).

— . 1964. *L'usure par l'existence* (Paris, Masson).

— . 1974. *Stress, fatigue, dépression* (Paris, Doin), 2 vols.

Burger, G. C. E.; Van Alphen de Veer, M. R.; Groot Wesseldijk, A. Th.; Van der Graaf, M. H. K.; Doornbosch, A. 1958. "Human problems in shift work", in *Proceedings of the XII International Congress on Occupational Health, Helsinki, 1-6 July 1957* (Helsinki), pp. 126-128.

Caille, E. J. 1966. "Analyse spectrale de l'EEG dans les états de veille et de sommeil", in *Actes du 1er Congrès d'électronique médicale et de génie biologique* (Tours).

— ; Bock, G.; Goybet, P.; Requin, J.; Roman, C. 1968. "Problèmes méthodologiques posés par l'étude psychophysiologique du niveau d'efficience dans les tâches de guidage", in *Actes du 3e Congrès d'ergonomie de langue française* (Brussels, Presses universitaires), pp. 97-105.

Caillot, R. 1959. "Conséquences sociales du travail à feu continu", in *Economie et humanisme* (Caluire, France), No. 122, pp. 62-72.

Carpentier, J. 1969. *Le travail en équipes alternantes : ses incidences professionnelles, individuelles et sociales* (Paris, Société nationale des pétroles d'Aquitaine).

— . 1974. "Organisational techniques and the humanisation of work", in *International Labour Review* (Geneva, ILO), Aug. 1974.

— ; Wisner, A. 1976. *L'aménagement des conditions du travail posté*. Report prepared at the request of the Ministry of Labour (Paris, Agence nationale pour l'amélioration des conditions de travail).

— . See also INRS.

Chalendar, J. de. 1973. *New patterns for working time : International conference, Paris, 26th-29th September 1972 : Final report* (Paris, OECD).

Chauchard, P. 1962. *La fatigue* (Paris, PUF).

Chazalette, A. 1973. *Une étude sur les conséquences du travail en équipes alternantes et leurs facteurs explicatifs* (Lyon, Groupe de sociologie urbaine).

Chevrolle, J. 1963. "Horaires de travail et infarctus du myocarde chez les employés de l'Assistance publique", in *Arch. mal. prof.*, Vol. 24, Nos. 1, 2, 3, pp. 146-147.

Club of Rome, Executive Committee. 1974. *Le rapport de Tokyo sur l'homme et la croissance*, collection "Equilibres" (Paris, Seuil).

Colquhoun, W. P.; Blake, M. J. F.; Edwards, R. S. 1968. "Experimental studies of shift-work I: A comparison of 'rotating' and 'stabilized' 4-hour shift systems", in *Ergonomics* (London, Taylor and Francis), Sep. 1968, pp. 437-453.

Confédération française démocratique du travail (CFDT), Fédération unifiée des industries chimiques. 1974. *Le travail "posté"* (Paris).

Crespy, J. 1974. "Médicaments et conduite automobile: état du problème", in *Le travail humain* (Paris, PUF), Vol. 37, No. 1, pp. 1-22.

Demaret, D.; Fialaire, J. 1974. "L'ulcère gastro-duodénal en milieu de travail: sa relation possible avec le régime des 3 × 8", in *Arch. mal. prof.*, Vol. 35, No. 3.

Dement, W. 1960. "The effect of dream privation", in *Science* (Washington, DC, American Association for the Advancement of Science), Vol. 131, No. 3415, 10 June 1960, pp. 1705-1707.

Dervillée, P.; Lazarini, M. J. 1959. "A propos du travail en équipes avec changement d'horaire: incidences familiales et répercussions possibles sur la santé des travailleurs", in *Arch. mal. prof.*, Vol. 20, pp. 306-309.

Durafour, M. 1976. Statement made as Minister of Labour for France, in an interview by Ph. Dumont, in *Le Monde* (Paris), 17 July 1976.

Ehrenstein, W.; Müller-Limmroth, W. 1975. "Changes in sleep patterns caused by shift work and traffic noise", in *Int. J. Chronobio.*, pp. 13-14.

Euler, U. S. von. 1953. "Adrenalin and noradrenalin in various kinds of stress", in *Symposium on stress* (Washington, DC, Army Medical Service Graduate School and Walter Reed Army Center).

Feinberg, I. 1969. "Effects of age on human sleep patterns", in A. Kales (ed.): *Sleep physiology and pathology : A symposium* (Philadelphia and Toronto, Lippincott), pp. 39-52.

Ferguson, D. 1973. "A study of occupational stress and health", in *Ergonomics* (London, Taylor and Francis), Sep. 1973, pp. 649-663.

Folkard, S. 1975. "The nature of diurnal variations in performance and their implications for shift work studies", in *Int. J. Chronobio.*, p. 16.

Forêt, J. 1973. *Sommeil et horaires de travail irréguliers*. Thesis for doctorate in engineering (Lille, Université des sciences et techniques).

Fourré, L. 1962. *Le travail en équipes alternantes*. Thesis for doctorate in medicine (Strasbourg).

Frankenhaueser, M.; Sterki, K.; Jarpe, G. 1962. "Psychophysiological relations in habituation to gravitational stress", in *Perceptual and Motor Skills* (Missoula, Mont., Southern Universities Press), Vol. 15, p. 63.

— ; Froeberg, J.; Mellis, I. 1965/66. "Subjective and physiological reactions induced by electrical shocks of varying intensity", in *Neuroendocrinology* (Basel and New York, Karger), Vol. 1, pp. 105-112.

— ; Pátkai, P. 1965. "Interindividual differences in catecholamine excretion during stress", in *Scandinavian Journal of Psychology* (Stockholm, Almqvist and Wiksell), No. 6, pp. 117-123.

Frazer, R. 1947. *The incidence of neurosis among factory workers* (London, Medical Research Council, Industrial Health Research Board), Report No. 90.

French, J. D.; Porter, R. W.; Cavanaugh, E. B.; Longmire, R. L. 1954. "Experimental observations on 'psychosomatic' mechanisms: I. Gastrointestinal disturbances", in *Archives of Neurology and Psychiatry* (Chicago, American Medical Association), Sep. 1954, pp. 267-281.

Gabersek, F.; Lille, F.; Scherrer, J. 1965. "Sommeil de jour d'un groupe de travailleurs de nuit", in *Actes du 3e Congrès d'ergonomie de langue française* (Brussels, Presses universitaires), pp. 315-318.

Gaultier, M.; Housset, P.; Martin, E. 1961. "Enquête sur les troubles gastriques en milieu industriel", in *Arch. mal. prof.*, Vol. 22, No. 3, pp. 129-134.

Gavrilescu, N.; Pafnote, M.; Vaida, I.; Mihaila, I.; Carstocea, L.; Luchian, O.; Popescu, P. 1966. "Control-board shift work turning every two days", in *15th International Congress on Occupational Health, Vienna, 19-24 September 1966* (Vienna, Verlag der Wiener Medizinischen Akademie), Vol. IV, pp. 103-106.

Ghata, J.; Halberg, F.; Reinberg, A.; Siffre, M. 1968. "Rythmes circadiens désynchronisés (17-hydroxycorticostéroïdes, température rectale, veille-sommeil) chez deux sujets adultes sains", in *Annales d'endocrinologie* (Paris, Masson), No. 29, p. 269.

Ginesta, E. 1974. *Etude de la fatigue de la quarantaine chez la femme salariée.* Thesis for doctorate in medicine (Bordeaux).

Goldstein, K. 1951. *La structure de l'organisme* (Paris, Gallimard).

Gouars, 1973. *Etude de l'adaptation de l'homme à un rythme de vie artificiel imposé : simulation d'une périodicité de trente heures* (Mont-de-Marsan, Laboratoire d'études médico-psychologiques des Armées).

Grandjean, E. 1969. *Précis d'ergonomie : organisation physiologique du travail* (Paris, Dunod).

Grossin, W. 1969. *Le travail et le temps* (Paris, Anthropos).

Guérin, J.; Durrmeyer, G. 1973. *Etude de la fatigue mentale industrielle* (Université de Paris I, Institut des sciences sociales du travail).

— ; Devèze, G. (1974). *Charge de travail et système de rotation : résultats de deux enquêtes sur la fatigue mentale chez les sidérurgistes soumis ou non aux horaires alternants.* Colloque sur les horaires alternants, 28-29 November 1974. Paris.

Halberg, F. 1960. "Temporal coordination of physiologic function", in *Biological clocks : Cold Spring Harbor Symposium on Quantitative Biology* (Cold Spring Harbor, NY, The Biological Laboratory), Vol. 25, pp. 289-310.

— ; Howard, R. B. 1958. "24 hour periodicity and experimental medicine: Examples and interpretations", in *Postgraduate Medicine* (Detroit, Henry Ford Hospital), July 1958, pp. 349-358.

Hartmann, E. 1970. "What sleep is good sleep?", in E. Hartmann (ed.): *Sleep and dreaming* (Boston, Mass., Little, Brown), pp. 59-70.

— ; Baekeland, F.; Zwilling, G.; Hoy, P. 1971. "Sleep need: How much sleep and what kind?", in *American Journal of Psychiatry* (Baltimore, Md., American Psychiatric Association), Feb. 1971, pp. 1001-1008.

Held, R. R. 1967. "La fatigue névrotique", in *La fatigue* (Toulouse, Privat).

Herman, B. 1975. *The optimal international division of labour* (Geneva, ILO).

Hesselgren, O.; Adamsson, H.; Johansson et al. 1948. *Treskiftarbetare och tunnelarbetare* (Stockholm, Marcus).

Hetman, F. 1974. *Society and the assessment of technology* (Paris, OECD).

Hildebrandt, G.; Rohmert, W.; Rutenfranz, J. 1975. "The influence of fatigue and rest periods on the circadian variation of error frequency in shift workers (engine drivers)", in *Int. J. Chronobio.*, p. 6.

Hogg, W. A. 1961. "Shift work, a hazard to health?", in *Medical Bulletin* (New York, Standard Oil Company), Mar. 1961, pp. 2-21.

Ilmarinen, J.; Klimt, F.; Rutenfranz, J. 1975. "Circadian variations of maximal aerobic power", in *Int. J. Chronobio.*, pp. 3-4.

Institut national de recherche et de sécurité (INRS), with the collaboration of J. Carpentier. 1975. *Le travail par équipes successives* (Paris).

International Labour Office (ILO). 1952. *General problems of hours of work in the chemical industries with particular reference to a comparison of day work and shift work*, Report III, Chemical Industries Committee, Third Session, Geneva.

— . 1974. *Bulletin of Labour Statistics.* World Population Year special edition (Geneva).

— . 1975 a. *Making work more human : Working conditions and environment.* Report of the Director-General to the International Labour Conference, 60th Session, 1975 (Geneva).

— . 1975 b. *Womanpower : The world's female labour force in 1975 and the outlook for 2000* (Geneva).

— . 1975 c. *Médecine du travail, protection de la maternité et santé de la famille.* Occupational safety and health series, No. 29 (Geneva).

— . See also: Carpentier, 1974; Herman, 1975; Kabaj, 1968; Lindörn, 1974; Maurice, 1975.

Johnson, L. C. 1974. "Les phases de sommeil sont-elles en relation avec le comportement au réveil?", in *Psychologie médicale* (Paris), Vol. 6, No. 1, pp. 63-90.

Jouvet, D. 1962. *La phase rhombencéphalique du sommeil : ses rapports avec l'activité onirique.* Thesis for doctorate in medicine (Lyon).

Kabaj, M. 1965. "Shift-work and employment expansion", in *International Labour Review* (Geneva, ILO), Jan. 1965, pp. 47-62.

— . 1968. "Shift work and employment expansion: Towards an optimum pattern", ibid., Sep. 1968, pp. 245-274.

Kalmus, H. 1940. "Diurnal rhythms in the *axolotl larva* and in *drosophila*", in *Nature* (London, Macmillan), 13 Jan. 1940, pp. 72-73.

Kalsbeek, J. W. H. 1965. "Mesure objective de la surcharge mentale: nouvelle application de la méthode des doubles tâches", in *Le travail humain* (Paris, PUF), Vol. 28, pp. 121-122.

Klein, V. 1965. *Women workers : Working hours and services.* Employment of special groups, No. 1 (Paris, OECD).

— . 1970. "Synchronisation and harmonisation of working hours with the opening and closing of social services, administrative offices, etc.", in OECD : *Employment of women : Regional Trade Union Seminar, Paris, 26-29 November 1968 : Final report* (Paris), pp. 239-253.

Kleitman, N. 1963. *Sleep and wakefulness* (Chicago and London, University of Chicago Press, revised and enlarged ed.).

Knauth, P.; Rutenfranz, J. 1975. "The effects of noise on the sleep of nightworkers", in *Int. J. Chronobio.*, p. 3.

Köhegyi, I.; Bédi, G. 1962. "Der Zusammenhang zwischen Alkoholgenuss und Unfällen im ungarischen Kohlenbergbau", in *Internationales Archiv für Gewerbepathologie und Gewerbehygiene* (West-Berlin), Vol. 19, No. 1, pp. 87-99.

Kogi, K.; Saito, Y. 1971. "A factor-analytic study of phase discrimination in mental fatigue", in *Ergonomics* (London, Taylor and Francis), Jan. 1971, pp. 119-127.

— ; Takahashi, M.; Onishi, N. 1975. "Experimental evaluation of frequent eight-hours versus less frequent longer night shifts", in *Int. J. Chronobio.*, pp. 14-15.

Kripke, D. F.; Cook, B.; Lewis, O. F. 1971. "Sleep of night workers: EEG recordings", in *Psychophysiology* (Detroit, Society for Psychophysiological Research), Vol. 7, pp. 377-384.

Kuhn, E. 1967. "Les aspects métaboliques de la privation de sommeil par rapport à la fatigue", in *La fatigue* (Toulouse, Privat).

Lafontaine, E.; Ghata, J.; Laverhne, J.; Courillon, J.; Bellinger, G.; Laplane, R. 1967. "Rythmes biologiques et décalages horaires: étude expérimentale au cours de vols commerciaux long-courriers", in *Concours médical* (Paris, Concours médical), Vol. 189, No. 19, pp. 3731-3740, and No. 20, pp. 3963-3970.

Landier, H.; Vieux, N. 1976. *Le travail posté en question*, with a preface by A. Wisner (Paris, Editions du Cerf).

Laplanche, J.; Brault. 1963. "Réflexions sur l'adaptation du personnel hospitalier de l'Assistance publique au service de veille", in *Arch. mal. prof.*, Vol. 24, Nos. 1, 2, 3, pp. 151-154.

Lecocq, J. 1963. "Au sujet de quelques facteurs susceptibles d'influencer l'action pathologique des horaires de travail en équipes tournantes 3 × 8", in *Arch. mal. prof.*, Vol. 24, Nos. 1, 2, 3, pp. 214-218.

Lecomte du Noüy, P. 1936. *Le temps et la vie* (Paris, Nouvelle Revue Française).

Leplat, J.; Schmidtke, H. 1968. *Travail mental et automatisation.* Etudes de physiologie et de psychologie du travail, No. 6 (Luxembourg, Commission of the European Communities).

Leuliet, S. 1963. "Douze années de travail posté 3 × 8", in *Arch. mal. prof.*, Vol. 24, Nos. 1, 2, 3, pp. 164-171.

Levi, L. 1965. "The urinary output of adrenaline and noradrenaline during different experimentally induced pleasant emotional states", in *Journal of Psychosomatic Research* (New York and Oxford, Pergamon Press), No. 8, pp. 197-198 (extracts); and *Psychosomatic Medicine* (New York, American Elsevier Publishing Co.), No. 27, pp. 80-85.

— . 1966. "Physical and mental stress reactions during conditions simulating combat", in *Försvarsmedicin* (Stockholm, Försvarets Sjukvårdsstyrelse), No. 2, pp. 3-8.

Lidén, L.; Wallander, J. 1959. *Skiftarbete i verkstadsindustrin* (Shift work in the mechanical industries) (Stockholm, Industrins Utrednings Institut).

Lille, F. 1967. "Le sommeil de jour d'un groupe de travailleurs de nuit", in *Le travail humain* (Paris, PUF), Vol. 30, pp. 85-97.

— ; Pottier, M.; Scherrer, J. 1968. "Influence chez l'homme des niveaux d'activité mentale sur les potentiels évoqués", in *Revue neurologique* (Paris, Masson), No. 118, pp. 476-480.

Lindörn, B. F. 1974. *Economic aspects of night work* (Geneva, ILO; mimeographed).

Loveland, N. T.; Williams, H. L. 1963. Article in *Perceptual and Motor Skills* (Missoula, Mont., Southern Universities Press), Vol. 11, p. 926.

Magoun, H. W. 1958. *The waking brain* (Springfield, Ill., Charles C. Thomas).

Mann, F. C.; Hoffmann, L. R. 1960. *Automation and the worker* (New York, Henry Holt).

Marris, R. I. 1966. "The economics of shift working", in *The benefits and problems of shift working*. A PERA symposium (London, Production Engineering Research Association of Great Britain), June 1966.

Mason, J. W.; Sachar, E. J.; Fishman, J. R.; Hamburg, D. A.; Handlon, J. H. 1965. "Corticosteroid responses to hospital admission", in *Archives of General Psychiatry* (Chicago, American Medical Association), No. 13, pp. 1-8.

Maurice, M. 1975. *Shift work* (Geneva, ILO).

— ; Monteil, C. 1965. *Vie quotidienne et horaires de travail : enquête psychosociologique sur le travail en équipes successives* (Université de Paris I, Institut des sciences sociales du travail).

Meers, A. (1974). *Signification du rythme nycthéméral pour la performance en situation industrielle*. Colloque sur les horaires alternants, Paris, 28-29 November 1974.

Menzel, W. 1950. "Physiologie und Pathologie des Nacht- und Schichtarbeiters", in *Arbeitsphysiologie* (Berlin, Springer), No. 14, pp. 304-318.

Metz, B.; Schaff, G.; Grivel, F. 1960. *Fatigue et sécurité* (Strasbourg, Centre d'études de physiologie appliquée au travail).

Mokrane, M. 1971. *Les horaires postés à l'ENEMA* (Etablissement national d'exploitation météorologique et aéronautique) (Alger-Daïr-el-Beida, ENEMA).

Mollet, C. 1974. *Etude du sommeil de jour chez le travailleur posté*. Thesis for doctorate in medicine (Lille).

Moruzzi, G. 1954. "The physiological projections of the brain stem reticular formation", in H. H. Jasper (ed.): *Brain mechanisms and consciousness* (Oxford).

Mott, E.; Mann, C.; McLoughlin, Q.; Warwick, P. 1965. *Shiftwork : The social, psychological and physical consequences* (Ann Arbor, Mich., University of Michigan Press).

Mouret, J. (1974). *Effets des horaires alternants sur les états de sommeil et leur pathologie*. Colloque sur les horaires alternants, Paris, 28-29 November 1974.

Mouton, A. 1960. *Aspects particuliers de l'adaptation du travail à l'homme en milieu saharien*. Thesis for doctorate in medicine (Lille).

Murrell, K. F. H. 1965. *Ergonomics : Man in his working environment* (London, Chapman and Hall). Published in the United States as *Human performance in industry* (New York, Reinhold).

National Board for Prices and Incomes (United Kingdom). 1970. *Hours of work, overtime and shift working* (London, Her Majesty's Stationery Office).

Ostberg, O.; Svensson, G. 1975. "Functional age and physical work capacity during day and night", in *Int. J. Chronobio.*, p. 11.

Pátkai, P. 1971. "Interindividual differences in diurnal variations in alertness, performance, and adrenaline excretion", in *Acta Physiologica Scandinavica* (Stockholm), No. 81, pp. 35-46.

— ; Pettersson, K.; Akerstedt, T. 1975. "The diurnal pattern of some physiological and psychological functions in permanent night workers and in men working on two-shift (day and night) systems", in *Int. J. Chronobio.*, p. 5.

Pincus, G. 1947. *Recent progress in hormone research* (New York, Academic Press), Vol. I.

— ; Romanoff, L. P.; Carlo, J. 1954. "The excretion of urinary steroids by men and women of various ages", in *Journal of Gerontology* (Washington, DC, Gerontological Society), Apr. 1954, pp. 113-132.

Pittendrigh, C. S. 1960. "Circadian rhythms and the circadian organization of living systems", in *Biological clocks : Cold Spring Harbor Symposium on Quantitative Biology* (Cold Spring Harbor, NY, The Biological Laboratory), Vol. 25, pp. 159-184.

Pternitis, C. 1969. *Etude des modifications du potentiel évoqué visuel au cours d'une tâche expérimentale de surveillance et après un travail industriel de surveillance de 8 heures* (Paris, Charbonnages de France).

— . 1972. *Mise en lumière objective de la fatigue mentale* (Paris, Charbonnages de France).

— . 1975 a. *Etude du sommeil de jour chez le travailleur posté.* Thesis for doctorate in medicine (Lille; also published by the Centre d'études et de recherches des Charbonnages de France, Paris).

— . 1975 b. *Téléenregistrement de l'activité électrique cérébrale en milieu industriel pendant un travail de surveillance : résultats préliminaires.* Paper presented to the Société d'électro-encéphalographie et de neurophysiologie clinique de langue française (Paris, Centre d'études et de recherches des Charbonnages de France).

Pugh, T. F.; McMahon, B. 1962. *Epidemiology findings in United States mental hospital data* (Boston, Mass., Little, Brown).

Quaas, M. 1969. "Probleme der Adaptation, Leistungsfähigkeit und Organisation der Schichtarbeit in der DDR", in A. Swensson (ed.): *Night and shiftwork* (Stockholm, Institute of Occupational Health), pp. 112-123.

Raab, W. 1968. "Correlated cardiovascular adrenergic and adrenocortical responses to sensory and mental annoyances in man", in *Psychosomatic Medicine* (New York, American Elsevier Publishing Co.), No. 30, pp. 809-818.

Reinberg, A. 1974. *Des rythmes biologiques à la chronobiologie* (Paris, Gauthier-Villars).

— ; Halberg, F.; Ghata, J.; Siffre, M. 1966. "Spectre thermique (rythme de la température rectale) d'une femme adulte saine avant, pendant et après son isolement souterrain de trois mois", in *Compte rendu à l'Académie des Sciences* (Paris), p. 262.

— ; Ghata, J. 1964. *Les rythmes biologiques.* Collection "Que sais-je?" (Paris, PUF; new edition in preparation).

Rey, P.; Gramoni, R.; Meyer, J. J. 1974. "La fréquence critique de fusion et la courbe de De Lange: application aux mesures de la fatigue nerveuse et de la performance visuelle", in *Le travail humain* (Paris, PUF), Vol. 37, No. 1.

Richta, R. 1969. *La civilisation au carrefour* (Paris, Anthropos).

Roessler, R.; Greenfield, N. S. 1962. *Physiological correlates of psychological disorder* (Madison, Wis.).

Rutenfranz, J.; Klimmer, F.; Knauth, P. 1975. "Desynchronisation of different physiological functions during three weeks of experimental nightshift with limited and unlimited sleep", in *Int. J. Chronobio.*, p. 2.

Sachar, E. J.; Finkelstein J.; Heiman L. 1971. "Growth hormone in depressive illness", in *Archives of General Psychiatry* (Chicago, American Medical Association), Vol. 25, No. 3, pp. 263-269.

— ; Halpers, F., et al. 1973. "Plasma and urinary testosterone levels in depressed men", ibid., Vol. 28, No. 1, pp. 15-18.

Scherrer, J., et al. 1967. *Physiologie du travail : ergonomie* (Paris, Masson).

— ; Lille, F.; Gabersek, V. 1968. *Etude électrophysiologique du sommeil de jour : rêve et conscience* (Paris, PUF).

Schmidtke, H. 1951. "Über die Messung der psychischen Ermüdung mit Hilfe des Flimmertests", in *Psychologische Forschung* (Berlin), No. 23, p. 409.

— . 1965. *Die Ermüdung : Symptome, Theorien, Messversuche* (Berne and Stuttgart, Verlag Hans Huber).

Selye, H. 1950. *The physiology and pathology of exposure to stress* (Montreal, Acta Inc.).

Siffre, M. 1963. *Hors du temps* (Paris, Julliard).

Simpson, H. W.; Lobban, M. C.; Halberg, F. 1970. "Arctic chronobiology: Urinary near 24-hour rhythms in subjects living on a 21-hour routine in the Arctic", in *Arctic Anthropology*, Vol. 7, No. 1, pp. 144-164.

Smith, M.; Vernon, H. M. 1928. "A study of the two-shift system in certain factories", in Medical Research Council, Industrial Fatigue Board: *Two studies on hours of work*, Report No. 47 (London, His Majesty's Stationery Office), pp. 17-35.

Smolensky, M. H.; Reinberg, A.; Lee, R. E.; McGovern, J. P. 1974. "Secondary rhythms related to hormonal changes in the menstrual cycle: Special reference to allergology", in M. Ferin et al. (eds.): *Biorhythms and human reproduction* (New York, Wiley), pp. 387-406.

Solovieva, V. P.; Gambashidze, G. M. 1960. Article on physiological data relating to the work and rest of workers employed exclusively on night shifts, in *Gigiyena Truda i Professionalnyye Zabolevaniya* (Moscow), No. 7, pp. 17-23.

Surry, J. 1971. *Industrial accident research (a human engineering appraisal)* (Toronto, Ontario Department of Labour, Labour Safety Council).

Takahashi, R. 1968. "Catecholamine metabolism and depression", in *Advances in Neurological Sciences* (Tokyo, Japan Publications Trading Co.), No. 12, pp. 870-873.

Tejmar, J. 1976. "Shift work round the clock in supervision and control", in *Applied Ergonomics* (Guildford, Surrey, IPC Science and Technology Press), Vol. 7, No. 2, pp. 66-74.

Thiis-Evensen, E. 1958. "Shift work and health", in *Industrial Medicine and Surgery* (Chicago, Industrial Medicine Publishing Co.), Oct. 1958, pp. 493-497.

Tsaneva, N.; Daleva, M. 1975. "Field study of the diurnal changes of the adrenal system", in *Int. J. Chronobio.*, p. 7.

Tune, G. S. 1969. "Sleep and wakefulness in 509 normal human adults", in *The British Journal of Medical Psychology* (London, Cambridge University Press), Vol. 42, pp. 75-80.

Uhlich, E. 1957. "Zur Frage der Belastung des arbeitenden Menschen durch Nacht- und Schichtarbeit", in *Psychologische Rundschau* (Göttingen, Verlag für Psychologie), No. 1, pp. 57-59.

Van Alphen de Veer, M. R. 1955. *Succès et échec dans l'industrie* (Amsterdam, Van Gorcum).

Viaud, G. 1947. "Le pouvoir réparateur du sommeil et sa mesure", in *Journal de psychologie normale et pathologique* (Paris, PUF), No. 40, pp. 195-231.

Webb, W. B.; Friedman, J. K. 1969. "Length of sleep and length of waking: Inter- relations in the rat", in *Psychonomic Science* (Austin, Tex., Psychonomic Journals), No. 17, pp. 14-15.

— ; Agnew, H. W. 1970. "Sleep stage characteristics of long and short sleepers", in *Science* (Washington, D.C., American Association for the Advancement of Science), No. 168, pp. 146-147.

Weitzman, E. D.; Schaumburg, H.; Fishbein, W. 1966. "Plasma 17-hydroxycorti-costeroid levels during sleep in man", in *Journal of Clinical Endocrinology and Metabolism* (Philadelphia, Lippincott), Feb. 1966, pp. 121-127.

Wever, R. 1975. "The circadian multi-oscillator system of man", in *Int. J. Chronobio.*, pp. 19-55.

Wild, H. W.; Theis, H. 1967. "Der Einfluss des Schichtbeginns auf die Unfallhäufig-keit", in *Glückauf* (Essen, Verlag Glückauf), 17 Aug. 1967, pp. 833-838.

Williams, R. L.; Karacan, I.; Hursch, C. J. 1974. *Electroencephalography (EEG) of human sleep : Clinical applications* (New York, John Wiley).

Wohlin, L. 1970. *Skogsindustrins strukturomvandling och expansionsmöjligheter* (Forestry industries: Structural changes and expansion potential) (Stockholm, Industrins Utrednings Institut).

Wyatt, S.; Marriott, R. 1953. "Night work and shift changes", in *British Journal of Industrial Medicine* (London, British Medical Association), July 1953, pp. 164-172.

Zung, W. W. 1965. "A self-rating depression scale", in *Archives of General Psychiatry* (Chicago, American Medical Association), Vol. 12, pp. 63-70.